Treasury of Christmas Recipes

Appetizers & Beverages

Cheese Pine Cones

Makes 12 to 16 appetizer servings

- 2 cups (8 ounces) shredded Swiss cheese
- 1/2 cup butter or margarine, softened
- 3 tablespoons milk
- 2 tablespoons dry sherry or milk
- 1/8 teaspoon ground red pepper
- 1 cup finely chopped blanched almonds
- 3/4 cup slivered blanched almonds
- 3/4 cup sliced almonds
- 1/2 cup whole almonds
    Fresh rosemary sprigs
    Assorted crackers

Beat cheese, butter, milk, sherry and red pepper in medium bowl until smooth; stir in chopped almonds.

Divide mixture into 3 equal portions; shape each into tapered ovals to resemble pine cones. Insert slivered, sliced and whole almonds into cones as shown in photo. Cover; refrigerate 2 to 3 hours or until firm.

Arrange cheese pine cones on wooden board or serving plate. Garnish tops with rosemary. Serve with assorted crackers.

Holiday Appetizer Puffs

Makes about 1 1/2 dozen appetizers

- 1 sheet frozen puff pastry, thawed (1/2 of 17 1/4-ounce package)
- 2 tablespoons olive or vegetable oil
    Toppings: grated Parmesan cheese, sesame seeds, poppy seeds, dried dill weed, dried basil, paprika, drained capers, green olive slices

Preheat oven to 425°F. Roll pastry on lightly floured surface to 13×13-inch square. Cut into shapes with cookie cutters (simple shaped cutters work best). Place on ungreased baking sheets.

Brush cut-outs lightly with oil. Decorate with desired toppings.

Bake 6 to 8 minutes or until golden. Serve warm or at room temperature.

Clockwise from top: Holiday Appetizer Puffs, Pesto Cheese Wreath (page 4), Cheese Pine Cones

Pesto Cheese Wreath

Makes 16 to 24 appetizer servings

Parsley-Basil Pesto* (recipe
follows)
3 (8-ounce) packages cream
cheese, softened
1/2 cup mayonnaise
1/4 cup whipping cream or
half-and-half
1 teaspoon sugar
1 teaspoon onion salt
1/3 cup chopped roasted red
peppers** or pimiento,
drained
Pimiento strips and Italian
flat leaf parsley leaves
(optional)
Assorted crackers and
vegetables

Prepare Parsley-Basil Pesto; set
aside. Beat cream cheese and
mayonnaise in small bowl until
smooth; beat in whipping cream,
sugar and onion salt.

Line 5-cup ring mold with plastic
wrap. Spoon half the cheese
mixture into prepared mold;
spread evenly. Spread Parsley-Basil
Pesto evenly over cheese; top with
chopped red peppers. Spoon
remaining cheese mixture over
peppers; spread evenly. Cover;
refrigerate until cheese is firm, 8
hours or overnight.

Uncover mold; invert onto serving
plate. Carefully remove plastic
wrap. Smooth top and sides of

wreath with spatula. Garnish with
pimiento strips and parsley leaves
as shown in photo, if desired.
Serve with assorted crackers and
vegetables.

Parsley-Basil Pesto

Makes about 1/2 cup

2 cups fresh parsley leaves
1/4 cup pine nuts or slivered
almonds
2 tablespoons grated
Parmesan cheese
2 cloves garlic
1 tablespoon dried basil
leaves
1/4 teaspoon salt
2 tablespoons olive or
vegetable oil

Process all ingredients except oil
in food processor or blender until
finely chopped. With machine
running, add oil gradually,
processing until mixture is
smooth.

Pineapple Mint Tulip

Makes 1 serving

1 cup DOLE® Pineapple Juice
2 tablespoons powdered
sugar
1 tablespoon grenadine
syrup
1 sprig fresh mint
Ice cubes or pineapple
juice cubes

In 1-quart measure, combine
pineapple juice, sugar and
grenadine; stir well. Rub mint
sprig around inside of tall glass.
Partially fill glass with ice cubes;
pour in juice mixture.

*One-half cup purchased pesto
may be substituted for Parsley-
Basil Pesto.*

**Look for roasted red peppers
packed in cans or jars in the
Italian food section of the
supermarket.*

Bruschetta

Bruschetta

Makes 6 appetizer servings

1 can (14½ ounces) DEL
   MONTE® Italian Recipe
   Stewed Tomatoes
1 to 2 cloves garlic, crushed
2 tablespoons chopped fresh
   basil *or* ½ teaspoon
   dried basil
1 baguette (6 inches) French
   bread, cut into ½-inch
   slices
1 tablespoon olive oil

Drain tomatoes, reserving liquid.
In small saucepan, boil reserved
liquid with garlic, 5 to 6 minutes,
stirring occasionally. Remove from
heat. Chop tomatoes; combine
with garlic mixture and basil.
Brush bread with oil. Broil until
golden. Top with tomato mixture;
serve immediately. Garnish with
basil leaves, if desired.

Raspberry Wine Punch

Spirited Coffee Lopez

Makes 5 cups

4 cups hot coffee
1/2 cup COCO LOPEZ® Cream
of Coconut
1/2 cup Irish whiskey
1 teaspoon vanilla extract
Whipped cream

In heat-proof pitcher, combine all
ingredients except whipped cream;
mix well. Pour into mugs; top
with whipped cream. Serve
immediately.

Raspberry Wine Punch

Makes 8 servings

1 package (10 ounces) frozen
red raspberries in syrup,
thawed
1 bottle (750 mL) white
zinfandel or blush wine
1/4 cup raspberry-flavored
liqueur
3 to 4 cups distilled water,
divided
Fresh cranberries
Empty 1/2 gallon milk or
juice carton
Sprigs of pine and tinsel

Process raspberries with syrup in
food processor or blender until
smooth; press through strainer,
discarding seeds. Combine wine,
raspberry purée and liqueur in
pitcher; refrigerate until serving
time. Rinse out wine bottle and
remove label.

Fully open top of carton. Place
wine bottle in center of carton.
Tape bottle securely to carton so
bottle will not move when adding
water. Pour 2 cups distilled water
into carton. Carefully push pine
sprigs, cranberries and tinsel into
water between bottle and carton
to form decorative design. Add
remaining water to almost fill
carton. Freeze until firm, 8 hours
or overnight.

Just before serving, peel carton
from ice block. Using funnel, pour
punch back into wine bottle. Wrap
bottom of ice block with white
cotton napkin or towel to hold
while serving.

Note: Punch may also be served in
a punch bowl if desired.

Spinach-Cheese Appetizers

Makes 5 dozen appetizers

- 1/4 cup olive oil
- 1/2 cup chopped onion
- 2 eggs
- 16 ounces (1 pound) feta cheese, drained and crumbled
- 3 (10-ounce) packages frozen chopped spinach, thawed
- 1/2 cup minced fresh parsley
- 1 teaspoon dried oregano, crushed *or* 2 tablespoons fresh oregano, chopped
  - Freshly grated nutmeg to taste
  - Salt and black pepper to taste
- 1 package (16 ounces) frozen phyllo dough, thawed to room temperature
- 2 cups margarine, melted

Preheat oven to 375°F. Heat oil over medium-high heat in small skillet. Add onion; cook and stir until translucent. Beat eggs in large bowl; stir in onion, feta cheese, spinach, parsley and oregano. Season with nutmeg, salt and pepper.

Remove phyllo from package; unroll and place on large sheet of waxed paper. Fold phyllo crosswise into thirds. Use scissors to cut along folds into thirds. Cover phyllo with large sheet of plastic wrap and damp clean kitchen towel. Lay 1 strip of phyllo at a time on a flat surface and brush with melted margarine. Fold strip in half lengthwise; brush with margarine again. Place rounded teaspoonful of spinach filling on 1 end of strip; fold over one corner to make triangle. Continue folding end to end, as you would fold a flag, keeping edges straight. Brush top with margarine. Repeat process until all filling is used.

Place triangles in a single layer, seam-side down, on baking pan. Bake 20 minutes or until lightly browned. Serve warm.

Spinach-Cheese Appetizers

Spiced Red Wine

Makes 14 servings

> **Grape Ice Ring**
> **(recipe follows)**
> $^1/_2$ **cup sugar**
> $^1/_2$ **cup water**
> **1 bottle (750 mL) Burgundy**
> **wine, chilled**
> **2 cups white grape juice,**
> **chilled**
> **1 cup peach schnapps,**
> **chilled**

Prepare Grape Ice Ring.

Combine sugar and water in small saucepan. Bring to a boil. Boil, stirring constantly, until sugar dissolves. Cool to room temperature. Cover; refrigerate until chilled, about 2 hours.

Combine wine, grape juice, schnapps and sugar syrup in punch bowl. Float Grape Ice Ring in punch.

Grape Ice Ring

> **2 pounds assorted seedless**
> **grapes (Thompson, Red**
> **Empress, etc.)**
> **Lemon leaves* (optional)**

Fill 4-cup ring mold with water to within $^3/_4$ inch of top. Freeze until firm, about 8 hours or overnight. Arrange clusters of grapes and leaves on ice as shown in photo; fill with water to top of mold. Freeze until solid, about 6 hours. To unmold, dip bottom of mold briefly in hot water.

*These nontoxic leaves are available in florist shops.

Spiced Red Wine with Grape Ice Ring

Herbed Spinach Cheese Ball

Makes 1²/₃ cups

> **1 (8-ounce) package light**
> **cream cheese, softened**
> $^1/_2$ **cup light garlic herb**
> **cheese spread**
> **2 tablespoons finely**
> **chopped green onion**
> **2 teaspoons Worcestershire**
> **sauce**
> $^1/_8$ **teaspoon ground red**
> **pepper**
> **1 (10-ounce) package frozen**
> **spinach, thawed and well**
> **drained**
> **2 tablespoons toasted sesame**
> **seed**
> **52 TRISCUIT® Wafers**

In small bowl, blend cream cheese and cheese spread until smooth; stir in green onion, Worcestershire sauce and red pepper. Mix in spinach until well combined. Shape into 4-inch ball. Wrap with plastic wrap; chill at least 2 hours. To serve, roll ball in sesame seed. Serve as a spread on wafers.

Chunky Chili Dip

Makes about 1½ cups

- ²/₃ cup DANNON® Plain Nonfat or Lowfat Yogurt
- ⅓ cup mayonnaise or salad dressing
- ¼ cup finely chopped green bell pepper
- ¼ cup chili sauce
- 2 tablespoons finely chopped green onion
- 1 tablespoon prepared horseradish
  Assorted fresh vegetable dippers

In medium bowl, combine yogurt, mayonnaise, bell pepper, chili sauce, green onion and horseradish; mix well. Cover; chill before serving. Serve with vegetable dippers.

Splendid Spinach Dip

Makes about 3 cups

- 2 cups DANNON® Plain Nonfat or Lowfat Yogurt
- 1 package (10 ounces) frozen chopped spinach, thawed and squeezed dry
- ⅓ cup finely chopped fresh onion
- 2 tablespoons reduced-calorie mayonnaise
- 1 package (1.4 ounces) instant vegetable soup mix
  Assorted fresh vegetable dippers

In medium bowl, combine yogurt, spinach, onion, mayonnaise and vegetable soup mix; mix well. Serve immediately or cover and chill up to 3 hours. Serve with vegetable dippers.

Clockwise from top: Chunky Chili Dip, Creamy Tarragon Dip, Splendid Spinach Dip

Creamy Tarragon Dip

Makes about 2 cups

- 1 cup DANNON® Plain Nonfat or Lowfat Yogurt
- 1 cup mayonnaise or salad dressing
- 1 tablespoon chopped green onion
- 1 tablespoon snipped fresh parsley
- 2 teaspoons lemon juice
- 1/2 teaspoon dried tarragon, crushed
  Dash freshly ground pepper
  Assorted fresh vegetable dippers

In medium bowl, combine yogurt, mayonnaise, green onion, parsley, lemon juice, tarragon and pepper; mix well. Cover; chill up to 24 hours before serving. Serve with vegetable dippers.

Hot Mulled Cider

Makes 16 servings

- 1/2 gallon apple cider
- 1/2 cup packed light brown sugar
- 1 1/2 teaspoons balsamic or cider vinegar
- 1 teaspoon vanilla
- 1 cinnamon stick
- 6 whole cloves
- 1/2 cup applejack or bourbon (optional)

Combine all ingredients except applejack in large saucepan; bring to a boil. Reduce heat to low; simmer, uncovered, 10 minutes. Remove from heat; stir in applejack. Pour into punch bowl.

Lemony Light Cooler

Lemony Light Cooler

Makes about 7 cups

- 3 cups dry white wine or white grape juice, chilled
- 1/2 to 3/4 cup sugar
- 1/2 cup REALEMON® Lemon Juice from Concentrate
- 1 (32-ounce) bottle club soda, chilled
  Strawberries, plum, peach or orange slices or other fresh fruit
  Ice

In pitcher, combine wine, sugar and ReaLemon® brand; stir until sugar dissolves. Chill. Just before serving, add club soda and fruit; serve over ice.

Clockwise from top right: Smoked Salmon with Cucumber Dill Sauce, Spicy Marinated Shrimp with Avocado Dip (page 16), Cajun Scallop Kabobs, Crumb-Topped Clams

Smoked Salmon with Cucumber Dill Sauce

Makes 20 to 24 appetizer servings

- ¼ **cup mayonnaise**
- ¼ **cup plain yogurt**
- ¼ **cup GOLDEN DIPT® Lemon Butter Dill Cooking Sauce**
- ½ **cup finely chopped, peeled and seeded cucumber**
- 2 **tablespoons chopped fresh parsley**
- 2½ **to 3 pounds smoked whole salmon or other smoked fish, chilled**
  Cucumber slices for garnish
  Toast points for garnish

Combine mayonnaise, yogurt, cooking sauce, chopped cucumber and parsley. Cover and chill until serving time. Place salmon on large platter garnished with cucumber slices and toast points. Serve sauce with chilled salmon.

Crumb-Topped Clams

*Makes about 36 clams or
24 oysters*

**3 pounds live steamer or
littleneck clams *or*
2 dozen oysters in the
shell, well scrubbed**
**4 slices bacon, cooked and
crumbled, reserve
2 tablespoons drippings**
**1/3 cup finely chopped green
onions**
**1/3 cup finely chopped fresh
parsley**
**1/2 teaspoon grated lemon
peel**
2 tablespoons lemon juice
1/8 teaspoon hot pepper sauce
1 cup cracker crumbs
**1/4 cup grated Parmesan
cheese**

For clams, tap clams and discard
any that do not close. Fill large
pot with 1/2 inch of water; bring to
a boil. Add clams; cover and steam
just until shells pop open, about 2
minutes. Transfer to baking sheet.
Discard top shells. Loosen clams
and replace in juices in bottom of
shells.

Preheat oven to 400°F. In medium
saucepan, cook and stir green
onion and parsley in reserved
bacon drippings until soft, about
1 minute. Remove from heat; add
lemon peel, lemon juice and hot
pepper sauce. Stir in cracker
crumbs, Parmesan cheese and
reserved bacon. Using teaspoon,
mound crumb mixture over clams,
pressing gently. Bake 5 minutes or
until crumbs are golden brown.

For oysters, shuck oysters. Arrange
on baking sheet. Prepare crumb
topping as directed and spoon
over oysters, pressing gently. Bake
at 400°F about 8 minutes or until
oysters are just cooked and crumbs
are golden brown.

Cajun Scallop Kabobs

Makes 15 to 20 kabobs

1 pound sea scallops
**1/2 cup GOLDEN DIPT® Cajun
Style Barbecue Sauce,
divided**
1 green bell pepper
1 red bell pepper
**1 jar (10 ounces) lightly
spiced cocktail onions**
**15 to 20 medium bamboo
skewers, soaked in water**

Marinate scallops in refrigerator in
1/4 cup barbecue sauce for 30
minutes. Cut each pepper into
1/2-inch squares. Remove scallops
from marinade. Arrange scallops
and vegetables on skewers,
alternating scallops, peppers and
onions. (Kabobs may be covered
and refrigerated up to 4 hours
before cooking.) Arrange kabobs
on broiler pan. Brush with
barbecue sauce. Broil until scallops
are opaque, approximately 4 to 5
minutes. Brush with remaining
barbecue sauce halfway through
cooking time.

Turkey-Cheese Surprises

Makes about 24 meatballs

1 pound ground turkey
¹/₂ cup stuffing mix
¹/₂ cup finely chopped tart apple
¹/₂ cup *plus* 2 tablespoons Parmesan cheese, divided
¹/₂ teaspoon poultry seasoning
Garlic salt to taste
Black pepper to taste
1 tablespoon butter or margarine
¹/₂ cup finely chopped onion
2 eggs
¹/₄ cup POLLY-O® Ricotta cheese
4 ounces POLLY-O® Mozzarella cheese, cut into ¹/₂-inch cubes
1 cup dry bread crumbs
Vegetable oil
Cranberry sauce
Orange slices for garnish

Combine turkey, stuffing mix, apple, 2 tablespoons Parmesan cheese and poultry seasoning in large bowl; season with garlic salt and black pepper. Heat butter in small skillet over medium-high heat. Add onion; cook and stir until onion is translucent. Add onion, eggs and ricotta cheese to turkey mixture; blend well. For each meatball, shape small amount of turkey around a cube of mozzarella cheese. Mix bread crumbs and remaining ¹/₂ cup of Parmesan cheese in large shallow dish. Roll cheese-filled meatballs in mixture to coat well. Heat ¹/₄ inch oil in large heavy saucepan over medium-high heat. Cook

meatballs, a few at a time, until brown on all sides, 4 to 5 minutes. Remove with slotted spoon; drain on paper towels. Serve with cranberry sauce; garnish if desired.

Coconut Snowball Cocoa

Makes 8 servings

1 pint vanilla ice cream
1 cup flaked coconut
¹/₂ cup unsweetened cocoa
1 quart milk
¹/₂ cup dark rum (optional)
³/₄ to 1 cup cream of coconut
1 teaspoon coconut extract
¹/₂ cup chocolate-flavored ice cream sauce (optional)
8 maraschino cherries (optional)

Scoop ice cream into 8 small balls; immediately roll in coconut. Place on waxed paper-lined baking sheet; freeze until ready to use.

Whisk cocoa into milk in large saucepan. Stir in rum, if desired, cream of coconut and coconut extract. Bring to a simmer over medium-high heat. Pour into 8 large heatproof mugs.

Float ice cream balls in cocoa. If desired, drizzle each ice cream ball with chocolate sauce and top with cherry.

Turkey-Cheese Surprises

Spicy Marinated Shrimp with Avocado Dip

Makes 50 to 75 marinated shrimp

2 ½ to 3 pounds large or
    medium raw shrimp,
    peeled and deveined
    GOLDEN DIPT® Cajun
    Style Shrimp and Crab
    Seasoning
1 cup **GOLDEN DIPT®** Cajun
    Style Barbecue Sauce
½ cup lemon juice, beer or
    lemon-flavored sparkling
    water
2 (6-ounce) containers frozen
    avocado dip, thawed

Cook shrimp with Shrimp and
Crab Seasoning according to
package directions; set aside.
Combine barbecue sauce and
lemon juice; pour over cooked
shrimp. Cover and refrigerate
several hours or overnight.
Remove shrimp from marinade
and serve with avocado dip using
cocktail picks.

Smoked Salmon Spread

Makes about 1¼ cups

2 (3-ounce) packages cream
    cheese, softened
3 ounces smoked salmon,
    finely chopped
1 tablespoon chopped fresh
    dill *or* 1 teaspoon dried
    dill weed
2 teaspoons lemon juice
¼ teaspoon hot pepper sauce
¼ cup **HELLMANN'S®** or **BEST
    FOODS®** Real Mayonnaise
    or Light Reduced Calorie
    Mayonnaise Dressing
    Belgian endive leaves
    Assorted party breads or
    crackers

In medium bowl, beat cream
cheese until smooth. Stir in
smoked salmon, dill, lemon juice
and hot pepper sauce until well
mixed. Stir in mayonnaise until
blended. Cover; chill. Spoon or
pipe onto Belgian endive leaves
or serve with party breads or
crackers. Garnish as desired.

Smoked Salmon Spread

Parmesan Puffs

Makes 10 appetizers

  1 egg white
  ¼ cup mayonnaise or salad
     dressing
  ¼ cup grated Parmesan
     cheese
  ¼ cup chopped green onion
  10 RYKRISP® crackers, any
     flavor
     Paprika

Preheat oven to 400°F. Beat egg
white at high speed of electric
mixer until soft peaks form. Fold
in mayonnaise, cheese and green
onion. Spread 1 tablespoon
mixture on each cracker. Sprinkle
with paprika. Place on baking
sheet. Bake 4 to 5 minutes or until
tops are puffy and light brown.

Nutty Swiss Spread

Makes 1½ cups

  1 package (8 ounces) cream
     cheese, softened
  ½ cup (2 ounces) shredded
     Swiss cheese
  1 tablespoon chopped chives
  1 tablespoon white wine
  2 teaspoons prepared
     horseradish
  ⅓ cup slivered almonds
     RYKRISP® crackers, any
     flavor

In medium bowl, beat cream
cheese, Swiss cheese, chives, wine
and horseradish until well
combined. Fold in almonds.
Refrigerate, covered, 1 hour. Let
stand 5 to 10 minutes before
serving. Serve with Seasoned,
Sesame or Natural RyKrisp®
crackers.

Santa's Special Malted Cocoa

Santa's Special Malted Cocoa

Makes about 4 cups

  2½ cups chocolate ice cream
  1½ cups milk
     6 tablespoons sugar
     3 tablespoons NESTLÉ®
        Cocoa
     3 tablespoons CARNATION®
        malted milk powder

In blender container, combine all
ingredients. Cover; blend until
smooth. Serve immediately.

Swiss 'n' Cheddar Cheeseball

Makes 24 appetizer servings

- 1 package (8 ounces) cream cheese, softened
- 1/2 cup DANNON® Plain Nonfat or Lowfat Yogurt
- 2 cups shredded Swiss cheese (8 ounces)
- 2 cups shredded Cheddar cheese (8 ounces)
- 1/2 cup finely chopped onion
- 1/2 cup finely chopped pecans, divided
- 1 jar (2 ounces) diced pimiento, undrained
- 2 tablespoons sweet pickle relish
- 10 slices bacon, crisp-cooked, drained, crumbled and divided
- 1/4 cup snipped fresh parsley
- 1 tablespoon poppy seeds
  Assorted crackers

In large bowl, beat cream cheese and yogurt until fluffy. Beat in Swiss cheese, Cheddar cheese, onion, 1/4 cup pecans, undrained

Swiss 'n' Cheddar Cheeseball

pimiento, pickle relish and half the bacon. If desired, season with salt and pepper. Cover; chill until firm. Shape into 1 large or 2 small balls on waxed paper; set aside.

In small bowl, combine remaining bacon, remaining 1/4 cup pecans, parsley and poppy seeds; turn out onto clean sheet of waxed paper. Roll ball in bacon mixture to coat. Cover in plastic wrap; chill. Serve with crackers.

Glazed Chicken Wings

Makes 32 appetizers

- 1 (8-ounce) can jellied cranberry sauce
- 1/4 cup water
- 3/4 cup GREY POUPON® Specialty Mustard: Honey
- 1 teaspoon grated orange peel
- 16 chicken wings, split with tips removed (about 3 pounds)

In small saucepan, over low heat, heat cranberry sauce and water, stirring occasionally until blended. Stir in mustard and orange peel. Remove from heat; cool slightly. In medium bowl, mix chicken with mustard mixture; cover and chill several hours or overnight.

Preheat oven to 400°F. Remove chicken from marinade; reserve marinade. Arrange chicken on lightly greased foil-lined pan. Bake 40 to 45 minutes, turning and brushing chicken with marinade after 20 minutes.

Banana Nog

Makes 6 servings

2 cups milk
1 large ripe banana, cut into pieces
1/2 cup sugar
1 tablespoon cornstarch
2 egg yolks*
2/3 cup light rum
1/4 cup creme de cacao
1 teaspoon vanilla
2 cups half-and-half, chilled
Whipped cream
Unsweetened cocoa
6 miniature candy canes

Process milk and banana in blender or food processor until smooth. Mix sugar and cornstarch in medium saucepan; stir in milk mixture. Heat to simmering over medium heat, stirring occasionally.

Lightly beat egg yolks in small bowl; whisk about 1/2 cup milk mixture into egg yolks.

Whisk yolk mixture back into saucepan. Cook over medium heat, stirring constantly, until thick enough to coat the back of a spoon. *Do not boil.*

Remove from heat; stir in rum, liqueur and vanilla. Pour into large heatproof pitcher or bowl. Cover; refrigerate until chilled.

Just before serving, stir half-and-half into eggnog mixture. Serve in mugs or punch cups; garnish with dollops of whipped cream and a sprinkle of cocoa. Tie pieces of ribbon around candy canes; use as stirrers.

Use only grade A, clean, uncracked eggs.

Egg Champignons

Egg Champignons

Makes 8 appetizer servings

6 hard cooked eggs, peeled
1/4 cup dry bread crumbs
1/4 cup (1 ounce) crumbled blue cheese
2 tablespoons green onions, thinly sliced
2 tablespoons dry white wine
2 tablespoons butter, melted
1 tablespoon chopped fresh parsley *or* 1/2 tablespoon dried parsley flakes
1/2 teaspoon garlic salt
24 large fresh mushroom caps
Paprika (optional)
Green onions and tomato slices for garnish

Preheat oven to 450°F. Lightly grease baking sheet; set aside. Combine eggs, bread crumbs, blue cheese, 2 tablespoons green onion, wine, butter, parsley and garlic salt in medium bowl. Fill each mushroom cap with 1 rounded tablespoonful egg mixture. Place filled mushroom caps on prepared baking sheet. Bake 8 to 10 minutes. Sprinkle with paprika and garnish if desired.

Soups & Sides

Cranberry-Raisin Stuffing

Makes 7¹/₂ cups stuffing

- **12 slices cinnamon-raisin bread**
- **¹/₂ cup (1 stick) butter or margarine**
- **2 medium onions, chopped (2¹/₂ cups)**
- **1 teaspoon dried rubbed sage**
- **1 bag (12 ounces) fresh or partially thawed frozen cranberries, washed, picked through, coarsely chopped**
- **¹/₄ cup sugar**
- **¹/₄ to ¹/₂ cup chicken broth***

Toast bread. Stack several pieces of toast and cut into ¹/₂-inch cubes. Repeat until all toast is cubed. Place in large bowl; set aside. Melt butter in large skillet; add onions. Cook and stir until tender (about 10 minutes). Add sage; cook 1 minute more. In medium bowl, toss cranberries with sugar; set aside. Add onion mixture and sugared cranberries to bread cubes; mix well. Pour ¹/₄ cup chicken broth over bread cube mixture; mix until evenly moistened. Stuff body and neck of turkey and cook according to instructions given with turkey.

Herb Sauced Vegetables

Makes 4 servings

- **3 cups fresh vegetables, such as broccoli flowerets, cauliflowerets, sliced yellow squash, green beans, carrots and snow peas**
- **1 cup chicken broth**
- **¹/₂ cup prepared HIDDEN VALLEY RANCH® Original Ranch® salad dressing**
- **¹/₄ cup chopped parsley**

In large saucepan, steam vegetables separately over boiling chicken broth until crisp-tender, about 5 minutes for each batch. Transfer to heated serving dish. Warm salad dressing and spoon over vegetables. Sprinkle with parsley.

*If cooking stuffing outside of turkey, use ¹/₂ cup chicken broth and bake, covered, at 350°F for 45 minutes or until heated through.

Cranberry-Raisin Stuffing

20

Tomato French Onion Soup

In large saucepan, cook onions in butter about 10 minutes. Drain tomatoes reserving liquid. Chop tomatoes. Add tomatoes, reserved liquid, 2 cups water, consomme and sherry to onions. Bring to boil, skimming off foam. Reduce heat and simmer 10 minutes. Place soup in four broilerproof bowls; top with bread and cheeses. Broil until cheese is melted and golden.

Tomato French Onion Soup

Makes 4 (1¹/₄-cup) servings

4 medium onions, chopped
2 tablespoons butter or margarine
1 can (14¹/₂ ounces) DEL MONTE® Italian Recipe Stewed Tomatoes
Water
1 can (10¹/₂ ounces) condensed beef consomme
¹/₄ cup dry sherry
4 slices toasted French bread
1¹/₂ cups shredded Swiss cheese
¹/₄ cup grated Parmesan cheese

Lemon-Glazed Carrots and Rutabaga

Makes 8 servings

4 to 5 medium carrots (about 12 ounces)
1 small rutabaga (about 12 ounces)
¹/₂ cup water
2 tablespoons butter
1 tablespoon *each* brown sugar, lemon juice
¹/₂ teaspoon grated lemon peel
¹/₄ teaspoon *each* dillweed, salt

Cut carrots and rutabaga into julienne strips about 3 inches long. Place carrots, rutabaga and water in medium saucepan; cover and cook over medium heat 13 to 15 minutes. Meanwhile, heat butter, brown sugar, lemon juice, lemon peel, dillweed and salt in small saucepan over medium heat, 2 to 3 minutes. Add to vegetables and continue cooking 3 to 4 minutes, stirring occasionally or until vegetables are glazed and tender.

Favorite recipe from **National Live Stock and Meat Board**

Harvest Vegetable Scallop

Makes 6 servings

- 4 medium carrots, thinly sliced (about 2 cups)
- 1 package (10 ounces) frozen chopped broccoli, thawed and drained
- 1 can (2.8 ounces) DURKEE® French Fried Onions
- 5 small red potatoes, sliced 1/8 inch thick (about 2 cups)
- 1 jar (8 ounces) pasteurized processed cheese spread
- 1/4 cup milk
  Ground black pepper
  Seasoned salt

Preheat oven to 375°F. In 12 × 8-inch baking dish, combine carrots, broccoli and *1/2 can* French Fried Onions. Tuck potato slices into vegetable mixture at an angle. Dot vegetables evenly with cheese spread. Pour milk over vegetables; sprinkle with seasonings as desired. Bake, covered, at 375°F for 30 minutes or until vegetables are tender. Top with remaining onions; bake, uncovered, 3 minutes or until onions are golden brown.

Saucy Skillet Potatoes

Makes 6 to 8 servings

- 1 tablespoon MAZOLA® Margarine
- 1 cup chopped onion
- 1/2 cup HELLMANN'S® or BEST FOODS® Real Mayonnaise or Light Reduced Calorie Mayonnaise Dressing
- 1/3 cup cider vinegar
- 1 tablespoon sugar
- 1 teaspoon salt
- 1/4 teaspoon freshly ground pepper
- 4 medium potatoes, cooked, peeled and sliced
- 1 tablespoon chopped parsley
- 1 tablespoon crumbled cooked bacon or real bacon bits

In large skillet, melt margarine over medium heat. Add onion; cook 2 to 3 minutes or until tender-crisp. Stir in mayonnaise, vinegar, sugar, salt and pepper. Add potatoes; cook, stirring constantly, 2 minutes or until hot (do not boil). Sprinkle with parsley and bacon.

Harvest Vegetable Scallop

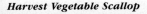

Apple & Dried-Cherry Chutney

Makes 2 cups

3 tablespoons vegetable oil
1 1/2 cups chopped red onion
1 tablespoon minced fresh
  ginger
1/4 teaspoon red pepper flakes
1/3 cup dried cherries
1 tablespoon dark brown
  sugar
1/4 teaspoon salt
1 cup water
1 Granny Smith apple, cored
  and finely chopped
1 teaspoon cornstarch,
  dissolved in 1 tablespoon
  water
1 teaspoon balsamic vinegar

In large skillet, heat oil over medium heat. Add red onion, ginger and pepper flakes; cook and stir 5 minutes. Add dried cherries, brown sugar, and salt. Stir in water; cover and cook over medium heat 5 minutes.

Add apple to onion mixture. Cover; cook 6 to 8 minutes or until apple is tender. Stir cornstarch mixture into apple-onion mixture and cook over high heat, stirring constantly, until mixture is thickened and appears glazed, about 1 minute. Remove from heat; stir in vinegar. Cool before serving or storing. Chutney can be refrigerated for one week or frozen for one month.

Favorite recipe from **Washington Apple Commission**

Easy Curried Corn Chowder

Makes 6 servings

1 can (16 ounces) California
  cling peach slices in
  juice or extra light syrup
1/2 pound bacon, cut into
  1-inch pieces
1 onion, thinly sliced
1/2 cup *each* chopped celery,
  sweet red and green bell
  peppers
1/4 cup all-purpose flour
2 teaspoons curry powder
1 package (10.5 ounces)
  frozen corn kernels,
  thawed
1 large potato, cut into
  1-inch cubes
2 (13 3/4-ounce) cans chicken
  broth
1 bay leaf
1 cup half-and-half

Drain peaches; cut slices in half and set aside. Cook bacon until brown in large saucepan over medium heat; remove from pan and drain on paper towels. Reserve. Drain drippings from pan reserving 2 tablespoons. Cook onion in reserved drippings about 8 minutes or until golden brown.

Stir in celery, peppers, flour and curry powder; cook 1 minute. Stir in corn, potato, broth and bay leaf. Bring to a boil, stirring frequently. Cover and simmer 20 minutes or until potatoes are tender. Remove from heat. Remove bay leaf; stir in half-and-half and reserved peaches. Ladle soup into serving bowls. Top with reserved crisp bacon just before serving.

Favorite recipe from **Canned Fruit Promotion Service**

Orange-Berry Salad

Makes 8 servings

- ¹/₂ cup prepared HIDDEN VALLEY RANCH® Original Ranch® salad dressing
- 2 tablespoons orange juice
- 1 teaspoon grated orange peel
- ¹/₂ cup heavy cream, whipped
- 1 can (11 ounces) mandarin orange segments
- 2 (3-ounce) packages strawberry- or raspberry-flavored gelatin
- 1 can (16 ounces) whole-berry cranberry sauce
- ¹/₂ cup walnut pieces
  Mint sprigs
  Whole fresh strawberries and raspberries

In large bowl, whisk together salad dressing, orange juice and peel. Fold in whipped cream; cover and refrigerate. Drain oranges, reserving juice. Add water to juice to measure 3 cups; pour into large saucepan and bring to boil. Stir in gelatin until dissolved. Cover and refrigerate until partially set. Fold orange segments, cranberry sauce and walnuts into gelatin. Pour into lightly oiled 6-cup ring mold. Cover and refrigerate until firm; unmold. Garnish with mint, fresh strawberries and raspberries. Serve with chilled dressing.

Orange-Berry Salad

Pumpkin Almond Bisque in Its Own Shell

Makes about 8 servings

  1 medium-size pumpkin
  3 cups chicken broth, divided
  2 tablespoons butter or margarine
  3 tablespoons chopped celery
  3 tablespoons chopped onion
  2 tablespoons almond paste
  1 tablespoon tomato paste
1½ cups light cream
  3 tablespoons almond-flavored liqueur
  1 teaspoon ground nutmeg
  1 teaspoon pepper
    Salt to taste
    Toasted Pumpkin Seeds (recipe follows)

Cut slice from top of pumpkin. Scoop out flesh, leaving shell that can be used for serving. Simmer pumpkin flesh in small amount of broth until tender. Place cooked pumpkin in food processor or blender container; process until smooth. (There should be 2 cups of pumpkin purée.) Leave purée in food processor.

Melt butter in heavy soup pot. Add celery and onion; cook over low heat 5 minutes. Add celery mixture, almond paste and tomato paste to pumpkin purée; process until smooth. Return contents of food processor to pot, add remaining broth and simmer over low heat, 30 minutes. Stir in cream and cook until heated

Pumpkin Almond Bisque in Its Own Shell

through. Stir in liqueur, nutmeg, pepper and salt. Pour into reserved pumpkin shell. Garnish with Toasted Pumpkin Seeds.

Toasted Pumpkin Seeds:
Carefully separate the pumpkin seeds from fibers. Wash, drain and dry on paper towels. Coat the seeds with small amount of vegetable oil. Add 2 tablespoons Worcestershire sauce and ½ teaspoon ground red pepper; toss to mix thoroughly. Spread seasoned seeds in single layer on baking sheet. Bake in 275°F oven, stirring occasionally, until golden brown.

Baked Apple & Sweet Potato Casserole

Makes 6 servings

  6 sweet potatoes
  3 apples
  2 tablespoons melted butter
 ½ cup orange juice
 ¼ cup packed dark brown sugar
 ⅛ teaspoon cinnamon
 ⅛ teaspoon allspice
 ¼ cup rum

Preheat oven to 350°F. Boil or steam potatoes until tender. Remove skin and cut lengthwise into slices. Peel and core apples and slice into rings. Butter 9×6-inch baking dish with 1 tablespoon butter and alternate potato and apple layers until dish is filled. Pour combined orange juice, sugar, seasonings, rum and remaining 1 tablespoon butter over potato mixture. Bake 30 minutes or until brown and shiny and the liquid is absorbed.

Favorite recipe from **Michigan Apple Committee**

Golden Apple-Sausage Dressing

Makes about 7 cups

- 1/2 **pound ground pork sausage**
- 1 **cup** *each* **chopped onion, celery**
- 8 **cups (3/4-inch) white bread cubes**
- 3 **cups (about 3 apples) chopped Golden Delicious apples**
- 1/4 **cup chopped parsley**
- 2 **teaspoons** *each* **crushed thyme, salt**
- 1/2 **to 1 teaspoon sage, crushed**
- 1/4 **teaspoon rosemary, crushed**
  Chicken or turkey broth

Preheat oven to 325°F. In large skillet, brown sausage; drain, reserving drippings. Set sausage aside. Add onion and celery to drippings in skillet; cook and stir lightly. Stir in sausage, bread cubes, apples, parsley and seasonings; toss to mix thoroughly. Stir in just enough broth (about 1 1/3 cups) to moisten mixture. Turn into greased 2-quart baking dish. Bake 1 hour. (For moist dressing, cover while baking.)

Favorite recipe from **Washington Apple Commission**

Pasta Hoppin' John

Makes 6 to 8 servings

- 1 **pound bow ties, spirals, wagon wheels, or other medium pasta shape**
- 1 **tablespoon vegetable oil**
- 1 **medium onion, chopped**
- 1 **jalapeño pepper, seeded and chopped**
- 3 **cloves garlic, chopped**
- 1 **green bell pepper, seeded and chopped**
- 1 **(28-ounce) can crushed tomatoes**
- 1 **(16-ounce) can black-eyed peas, rinsed and drained**
- 3 **tablespoons fresh chopped cilantro**
- 1 **tablespoon cider vinegar**
  Salt and black pepper to taste

Cook pasta according to package directions; drain. In large skillet, heat oil over medium heat. Cook and stir onion, jalapeño, garlic and bell pepper until softened; about 3 minutes. Add tomatoes; simmer 10 minutes, stirring occasionally. Add black-eyed peas, cilantro and vinegar; simmer 10 minutes more. Season with salt and black pepper. Toss with cooked pasta; serve immediately.

Favorite recipe from **National Pasta Association**

Golden Apple-Sausage Dressing

Oyster Stew

Oyster Stew

Makes 8 servings

1/4 cup (1/2 stick) butter
1 1/2 cups sliced mushrooms
1/2 cup chopped onion
1/4 cup all-purpose flour
1 teaspoon *each* salt,
    Worcestershire sauce
1/4 teaspoon white pepper
1 pint shucked oysters,
    liquid reserved
4 cups milk, scalded
2 cups light cream *or* half
    and half
    Lemon slices
    Chopped fresh parsley

Melt butter in large saucepan over
low heat; add mushrooms and
onion. Cook and stir until tender,
3 to 5 minutes. Stir in flour, salt,
Worcestershire sauce and pepper;
cook until bubbly. Stir in oysters
with liquid. Add milk. Cook until
simmering and oyster edges curl.
Stir in cream. Heat through.
Garnish with lemon slices and
parsley. Serve immediately.

Favorite recipe from **American Dairy
Industry Association**

Sweet Potato-Cranberry Bake

Makes 4 to 6 servings

1 can (40 ounces) whole
    sweet potatoes, drained
1 can (2.8 ounces) DURKEE®
    French Fried Onions
2 cups fresh cranberries
2 tablespoons packed brown
    sugar
1/3 cup honey

Preheat oven to 400°F. In 1 1/2-
quart casserole, layer sweet
potatoes, *1/2 can* French Fried
Onions and *1 cup* cranberries.
Sprinkle with brown sugar; drizzle
with *half* the honey. Top with
remaining cranberries and honey.
Bake, covered, at 400°F for 35
minutes or until heated through.
Gently stir casserole. Top with
remaining onions; bake,
uncovered, 1 to 3 minutes or until
onions are golden brown.

Corn Pudding

Makes 8 to 10 servings

> Peppered Beef Tip Roast (page 41)
> 1 bag (20 ounces) frozen whole kernel corn, thawed
> 1 small onion, quartered
> 2 cups milk
> 2 eggs, beaten
> 1 package (8½ ounces) corn muffin mix
> ½ teaspoon salt
> 1 cup shredded Cheddar cheese
> 1 cup thinly sliced romaine lettuce
> ½ cup julienned radishes

Prepare Peppered Beef Tip Roast. Combine corn and onion in food processor; cover and process using on/off pulse until corn is broken but not puréed, scraping side of bowl as necessary. Add milk and eggs; pulse until just blended. Add muffin mix and salt; pulse only until mixed. Pour mixture into greased 11¾ × 7½-inch baking dish. Bake with roast during last 45 to 50 minutes of cooking time or until outside crust is golden brown. Sprinkle pudding with cheese; place under broiler 3 to 4 inches from heat. Broil until cheese is melted and top is crusty. To serve, top with romaine lettuce and radishes.

Favorite recipe from **National Live Stock and Meat Board**

Savory Onion Tart

Makes about 8 servings

> Pastry for 9-inch single-crust pie
> ¼ cup WISH-BONE® Italian Dressing
> 2 tablespoons butter or margarine
> 2 large onions, thinly sliced
> 1 cup shredded fontina or Gruyere cheese (about 4 ounces)
> 2 eggs
> ½ cup whipping or heavy cream
> 2 teaspoons fresh sage leaves, finely chopped *or* ½ teaspoon dried sage leaves
> 1 teaspoon dried marjoram leaves
> ⅛ teaspoon pepper

Preheat oven to 425°F.

Roll pastry into 10-inch circle. Press into 9-inch tart pan and crimp edges tightly. Pierce bottom and side with fork. Bake 8 minutes or until lightly golden. Remove to wire rack and cool completely.

Meanwhile, in large skillet, heat Italian dressing with butter and cook onions over medium heat, stirring occasionally, 15 minutes or until onions are tender. Fill prepared tart shell with cheese, then onion mixture. In small bowl, beat eggs with cream, sage, marjoram and pepper; slowly pour over onion mixture. Bake 35 minutes or until golden. To serve, cut into wedges.

Pine Nut Dressing

Pine Nut Dressing

Makes 6 servings

   1 bag SUCCESS® White or
      Brown Rice
   1 tablespoon reduced-calorie
      margarine
 1/2 cup chopped onion
 1/2 cup chopped celery
 1/4 cup pine nuts, toasted
   1 tablespoon chopped fresh
      parsley
 3/4 teaspoon poultry
      seasoning
 1/4 teaspoon celery salt
 1/4 teaspoon pepper
 1/2 cup low-sodium chicken
      broth

Prepare rice according to package
directions.

Melt margarine in large saucepan
over medium heat. Add onion and
celery; cook and stir until crisp-
tender. Stir in rice and remaining
ingredients. Reduce heat to low;
simmer 10 minutes, stirring
occasionally.

Entrées

Baked Ham with Sweet and Spicy Glaze

Makes 8 to 10 servings

1 (8-pound) bone-in smoked half ham
Sweet and Spicy Glaze (recipe follows)

Preheat oven to 325°F. Place ham, fat side up, on rack in roasting pan. Insert meat thermometer with bulb in thickest part away from fat or bone. Roast ham in oven about 3 hours.

Prepare Sweet and Spicy Glaze. Remove ham from oven; do not turn oven off. Generously apply glaze over ham; return to oven 30 minutes longer or until meat thermometer registers internal temperature of 160°F. Remove ham from oven and reglaze. Let ham sit about 20 minutes before slicing.

Sweet and Spicy Glaze

Makes about 2 cups

3/4 cup packed brown sugar
1/3 cup cider vinegar
1/4 cup golden raisins
1 can (8 3/4 ounces) sliced peaches in heavy syrup, drained, chopped, syrup reserved
1 tablespoon cornstarch
1/4 cup orange juice
1 can (8 1/4 ounces) crushed pineapple in syrup, undrained
1 tablespoon grated orange peel
1 garlic clove, crushed
1/2 teaspoon crushed red pepper flakes
1/2 teaspoon grated fresh ginger

Combine brown sugar, vinegar, raisins and peach syrup in medium saucepan. Bring to boil over high heat; reduce to low and simmer 8 to 10 minutes. In small bowl, dissolve cornstarch in orange juice; add to brown sugar mixture. Add remaining ingredients; mix well. Cook over medium heat, stirring constantly, until mixture boils and thickens. Remove from heat.

Baked Ham with Sweet and Spicy Glaze

Deep-Dish Turkey Pie

Makes 6 servings

> 3 cups cubed cooked turkey
>   or chicken
> 1 cup sliced cooked carrots
> 1 cup cubed cooked potatoes
> 1 cup frozen green peas,
>   thawed
> 6 tablespoons margarine or
>   butter
> 1/3 cup unsifted flour
> 2 tablespoons WYLER'S® or
>   STEERO® Chicken-Flavor
>   Instant Bouillon *or*
>   6 Chicken-Flavor
>   Bouillon Cubes
> 1/4 teaspoon pepper
> 4 cups BORDEN® or
>   MEADOW GOLD® Milk
> 2 1/4 cups biscuit baking mix

Preheat oven to 375°F. In large saucepan, melt margarine; stir in flour, bouillon and pepper. Over medium heat, gradually add milk; cook and stir until bouillon dissolves and mixture thickens. Add remaining ingredients except biscuit mix; mix well. Pour into 2 1/2-quart baking dish. Prepare biscuit mix according to package directions for rolled biscuits. Roll out to cover dish; cut slashes in center of dough. Place on top of dish; crimp edges. Bake 40 minutes or until golden. Refrigerate leftovers.

Horseradish-Herb-Crusted Leg of Lamb

Makes 10 servings

> 1 (6-pound) leg of lamb
> 2 cups fresh white bread
>   crumbs
> 1/3 cup chopped parsley
> 3 garlic cloves, minced
> 1 1/2 teaspoons dried rosemary
>   leaves
> 1 teaspoon dried thyme
>   leaves
> 1/2 cup BLUE BONNET®
>   75% Vegetable Oil
>   Spread, melted
> 1/3 cup GREY POUPON®
>   Specialty Mustard:
>   Horseradish

Preheat oven to 350°F. Remove fat from lamb with sharp knife. Place on rack in roasting pan. Bake 1 hour. Remove from oven; cool 10 to 15 minutes.

Combine crumbs, parsley, garlic, rosemary and thyme; blend in spread. Spread top and sides of lamb with mustard. Press crumb mixture evenly and firmly into mustard. Lightly cover with foil. Bake 30 minutes. Remove foil; bake 30 to 45 minutes more or until meat thermometer registers internal temperature of 140°F to 160°F, depending on desired doneness. Remove from oven and let stand 10 minutes before slicing.

Deep-Dish Turkey Pie

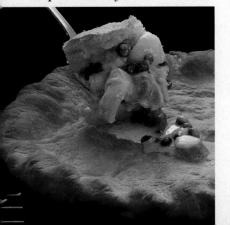

Honey Sesame Tenderloin

Honey Sesame Tenderloin

Makes 4 servings

- 1 pound whole pork tenderloin
- 1/2 cup soy sauce
- 2 cloves garlic, minced
- 1 tablespoon grated fresh ginger *or* 1 teaspoon ground ginger
- 1 tablespoon sesame oil
- 1/4 cup honey
- 2 tablespoons brown sugar
- 4 tablespoons sesame seed

Combine soy sauce, garlic, ginger and sesame oil. Place tenderloin in resealable plastic bag; pour soy sauce mixture over to coat. Marinate 2 hours or overnight in refrigerator. Preheat oven to 375°F. Remove pork from marinade; pat dry. Mix together honey and brown sugar on a plate. Place sesame seed on a separate plate. Roll pork in honey mixture, coating well; then roll in sesame seed. Roast in shallow pan 20 to 30 minutes, or until inserted meat thermometer registers 160°F. Remove to serving platter; slice thinly to serve.

Favorite recipe from **National Pork Producers Council**

Stuffed Chicken with Apple Glaze

Stuffed Chicken with Apple Glaze

Makes 4 servings

   1 broiler-fryer chicken
       (3 1/2 to 4 pounds)
 1/2 teaspoon salt
 1/4 teaspoon pepper
   2 tablespoons vegetable oil
   1 package (6 ounces)
       chicken-flavored stuffing
       mix, plus ingredients to
       prepare mix
   1 cup chopped apple
 1/4 cup chopped walnuts
 1/4 cup raisins
 1/4 cup thinly sliced celery
 1/2 teaspoon grated lemon
       peel
 1/2 cup apple jelly
   1 tablespoon lemon juice
 1/2 teaspoon ground cinnamon

Preheat oven to 350°F. Sprinkle inside of chicken with salt and pepper; rub outside with oil.

Prepare stuffing mix in large bowl according to package directions. Add apple, walnuts, raisins, celery and lemon peel; mix thoroughly. Stuff body cavity loosely with stuffing.* Place chicken in baking pan. Cover loosely with aluminum foil; roast 1 hour.

Meanwhile, combine jelly, lemon juice and cinnamon in small saucepan. Simmer over low heat 3 minutes or until blended. Remove foil from chicken; brush with jelly glaze. Roast chicken, uncovered, brushing frequently with jelly glaze, 30 minutes or until meat thermometer inserted into thickest part of thigh registers 185°F and juices run clear. Let chicken stand 15 minutes before carving.

Bake any leftover stuffing in covered casserole alongside chicken until heated through.

Favorite recipe from **Delmarva Poultry Industry, Inc.**

Baked Turkey Sandwich

Makes 10 servings

- 2 cups (10 ounces) diced cooked BUTTERBALL® Turkey
- 1/3 cup chopped SWIFT PREMIUM® Peperoni
- 1 loaf (16 ounces) frozen bread dough, thawed
- 3/4 cup (3 ounces) shredded Cheddar cheese
- 3/4 cup (3 ounces) shredded mozzarella cheese
- 3/4 cup chopped onion
- 1/2 cup chopped celery
- 1/3 cup mayonnaise
- 1/2 teaspoon salt
- 1/8 teaspoon ground black pepper
- 1 egg white
- 1 tablespoon water
  Sesame seeds

Let bread dough warm and start to rise. Preheat oven to 375°F. To make filling, combine turkey, peperoni, cheeses, onion, celery, mayonnaise, salt and pepper in medium bowl. On floured surface, roll dough into 15×11-inch rectangle. Place on greased cookie sheet. Spread filling lengthwise down center third of rectangle, leaving 1/2 inch on each end. Cut dough, on both sides of filling, crosswise at 1 1/2-inch intervals almost to filling. To enclose filling, take strip from each side, twist once and pinch ends together. Continue with remaining strips. Press each end of loaf together and fold under. Mix egg white and water; brush on dough. Sprinkle with sesame seeds. Bake 35 minutes or until golden brown. Let stand 10 minutes before slicing.

Pork Tenderloin Diane

Makes 4 servings

- 1 pound pork tenderloin, cut into 8 crosswise pieces
- 2 teaspoons lemon pepper
- 2 tablespoons butter
- 2 tablespoons lemon juice
- 1 tablespoon Worcestershire sauce
- 1 teaspoon Dijon-style mustard
- 1 tablespoon minced parsley or chives

Pound each tenderloin slice, with meat mallet, to 1-inch thickness; sprinkle with lemon pepper. Heat butter in heavy skillet; cook tenderloin medallions 3 to 4 minutes on each side or until fork-tender. Remove medallions to serving platter; keep warm. Add lemon juice, Worcestershire sauce and mustard to pan juices in skillet. Cook until heated through. Pour sauce over medallions and sprinkle with parsley; serve.

Favorite recipe from **National Pork Producers Council**

Pork Tenderloin Diane

Baked Stuffed Snapper

Makes 4 servings

> 1 red snapper (1½ pounds)
> 2 cups hot cooked rice
> 1 can (4 ounces) sliced mushrooms, drained
> ½ cup diced water chestnuts
> ¼ cup thinly sliced green onions
> ¼ cup diced pimiento
> 2 tablespoons chopped parsley
> 1 tablespoon grated lemon peel
> ½ teaspoon salt
> ⅛ teaspoon ground black pepper
> Vegetable cooking spray
> 1 tablespoon margarine, melted

Preheat oven to 400°F. Clean and butterfly fish. Combine rice, mushrooms, water chestnuts, onions, pimiento, parsley, lemon peel, salt and pepper; toss lightly. Fill cavity of fish with rice mixture; close with wooden toothpicks soaked in water. Place fish in 13×9-inch baking dish coated with cooking spray; brush fish with margarine. Bake 18 to 20 minutes or until fish flakes easily with fork. Wrap remaining rice in foil and bake in oven with fish.

Favorite recipe from **USA Rice Council**

Turkey with Garlic and Chili Pepper Stuffing

Makes 12 to 14 servings

> 1 (4- to 6-pound) BUTTERBALL® Turkey, thawed if frozen
> 2 medium red bell peppers, chopped
> ½ cup chopped onion
> 4 to 5 large cloves garlic, minced
> ⅓ cup butter or margarine
> 2 (4-ounce) cans diced green chili peppers, drained
> ¼ cup chopped fresh parsley
> ¼ teaspoon salt
> ¼ teaspoon ground red pepper
> 8 cups unseasoned dried whole wheat or white bread cubes
> 1½ cups (6 ounces) shredded Cheddar cheese
> ¾ to 1 cup chicken broth

Preheat oven to 325°F. To make stuffing, sauté red bell peppers, onion and garlic in butter in medium saucepan over medium-high heat until crisp-tender. Stir in chili peppers, parsley, salt and ground red pepper. Combine bread cubes, cheese and vegetable mixture in large bowl. Add enough broth to moisten. Toss to mix.

Prepare turkey for roasting, stuffing neck and body cavities lightly. Roast immediately, according to package directions or roast turkey unstuffed and place stuffing in greased 2½-quart casserole. Cover casserole and bake alongside turkey 1 hour or until hot.

Baked Stuffed Snapper

Turkey Breast Provençal with Vegetables

Makes 12 servings

1 cup turkey or chicken bouillon
¼ cup white wine
¼ cup lemon juice
1 head garlic, cloves separated, unpeeled
1 bag (10 ounces) frozen onions
2 teaspoons dried rosemary, crushed
1 teaspoon dried thyme, crushed
½ teaspoon salt
¼ teaspoon fennel seeds
¼ teaspoon ground black pepper
6 plum tomatoes, quartered
1 package (9 ounces) frozen artichoke hearts, slightly thawed
1 package (10 ounces) frozen asparagus spears, slightly thawed
1 can (3¼ ounces) pitted ripe olives, drained
1 bone-in (4½ pound) turkey breast

1. In 13×9-inch baking pan combine bouillon, wine, lemon juice, garlic, onions, rosemary, thyme, salt, fennel seeds and black pepper. Cover pan with foil. Bake 20 minutes at 325°F.

2. Remove pan from oven. Add tomatoes, artichoke hearts, asparagus and olives. Place turkey breast on top of vegetables. Cover and bake 1 hour. Remove foil and bake 1 hour or until meat thermometer inserted in thickest part of breast registers 170°F. Baste turkey and vegetables frequently with pan juices.

3. Remove turkey and vegetables to serving platter. Reserve 6 cloves of garlic and pan juices.

4. Remove skin from reserved garlic. Combine with pan juices in food processor bowl, fitted with metal blade. Process 30 to 60 seconds until mixture is smooth.

5. Serve sauce with turkey and vegetables.

Favorite recipe from **National Turkey Federation**

Turkey Breast Provençal with Vegetables

Peppered Beef Tip Roast with Corn Pudding (page 30)

Peppered Beef Tip Roast with Corn Pudding

- 1 (3½- to 5-pound) beef tip roast
- 2 teaspoons *each* cracked black pepper, dry mustard
- ½ teaspoon *each* ground allspice, red pepper
- 1 large garlic clove, minced
- 1 teaspoon vegetable oil
- Corn Pudding (recipe page 30)

Combine black pepper, dry mustard, allspice, red pepper and garlic; stir in oil to form paste.

Spread mixture evenly on surface of beef tip roast. Place roast, fat side up, on rack in open roasting pan. Insert meat thermometer so bulb is centered in thickest part. Do not add water. Do not cover. Roast in 325°F oven to desired doneness. Allow 30 to 35 minutes per pound. Meanwhile, prepare Corn Pudding. Remove roast when meat thermometer registers 135°F for rare; 155°F for medium. Allow roast to stand 15 to 20 minutes in a warm place for carving. Roasts continue to rise about 5°F in temperature to reach 140°F for rare; 160°F for medium. Serve carved roast with Corn Pudding.

Favorite recipe from **National Live Stock and Meat Board**

Coq au Vin

Coq au Vin

Makes 4 to 6 servings

4 thin slices bacon, cut into
   ¹/₂-inch pieces
6 chicken thighs, skinned
³/₄ teaspoon dried thyme,
   crushed
1 large onion, coarsely
   chopped
4 cloves garlic, minced
¹/₂ pound small red potatoes,
   quartered
10 mushrooms, quartered
1 can (14¹/₂ ounces) DEL
   MONTE® Italian Recipe
   Stewed Tomatoes
1¹/₂ cups dry red wine

In 4-quart heavy saucepan, cook bacon until just starting to brown. Sprinkle chicken with thyme; season with salt and pepper, if desired. Add chicken to pan; brown over medium-high heat. Add onion and garlic. Cook 2 minutes; drain. Add potatoes, mushrooms, tomatoes and wine. Cook, uncovered, over medium-high heat about 25 minutes or until potatoes are tender and sauce thickens, stirring occasionally. Garnish with chopped parsley, if desired.

Lemon-Ginger-Prune Veal Roll

Makes 10 servings

- 1 cup chopped prunes
- 1 tablespoon finely shredded lemon peel
- 1 tablespoon grated fresh ginger
- 1 (4- to 4½-pound) boneless veal breast
- ½ teaspoon salt
- 2 teaspoons vegetable oil
- ⅔ cup Madeira
- ⅓ cup water
   Lemon wedges

In small bowl, combine prunes, lemon peel and ginger. Unroll boneless veal breast; trim fat. Sprinkle evenly with salt. Distribute prune mixture evenly over surface. Roll up veal breast; tie securely with string. Heat oil in Dutch oven just large enough to hold veal. Brown veal on all sides. Drain excess fat if necessary. Add Madeira and water to pan; cover tightly. Cook in 325°F oven until tender, 2 to 2½ hours. Transfer to warm platter; let stand. Skim fat from pan juices. Place Dutch oven over direct heat. Bring pan juices to a boil and cook until reduced by half. Slice veal roll; discard strings. Spoon sauce over each serving. Garnish with lemon wedges.

Favorite recipe from **National Live Stock and Meat Board**

Beef Tenderloin au Poivre

Makes 6 servings

- 1 (3- to 3½-pound) beef tenderloin roast
- ⅔ cup Rhine wine
- ⅓ cup vegetable oil
- 1 small onion, chopped
- 1 clove garlic, minced
- 1½ teaspoons salt
- 1 to 2 tablespoons cracked black pepper

For marinade, combine wine, oil, onion, garlic and salt. Place beef tenderloin roast in resealable plastic bag. Add marinade, turning to coat. Seal bag and marinate in refrigerator 6 to 8 hours or overnight. Remove tenderloin from marinade; pat dry with paper towel. Roll roast in cracked pepper, lightly pressing onto surface of beef. Place tenderloin on rack in roasting pan. Do not add water. Do not cover. Insert meat thermometer so bulb is centered in thickest part. Roast in 425°F oven until meat thermometer registers 135°F (about 45 to 50 minutes). Let stand 15 minutes. Carve into thin slices.

Favorite recipe from **National Live Stock and Meat Board**

Lemon-Ginger-Prune Veal Roll

Almond Butter Chicken

Makes 4 servings

> 2 boneless skinless chicken
> breasts, halved (about
> 1¼ pounds)
> 2 tablespoons all-purpose
> flour
> ½ teaspoon salt
> ½ teaspoon pepper
> 1 egg, beaten
> 1 package (2¼ ounces)
> sliced almonds
> ¼ cup butter
> Orange Sauce (recipe
> follows)

Place each chicken breast half between 2 pieces of plastic wrap. Pound to ¼-inch thickness. Coat chicken with flour. Sprinkle with salt and pepper. Dip one side of each chicken breast into egg; press with almonds. Melt butter in large skillet over medium high heat. Cook chicken, almond side down, 3 to 5 minutes or until almonds are toasted; turn chicken over. Reduce heat to medium-low; cook 10 to 12 minutes or until chicken is tender and juices run clear. Serve, almond side up, with Orange Sauce. Garnish as desired.

Almond Butter Chicken

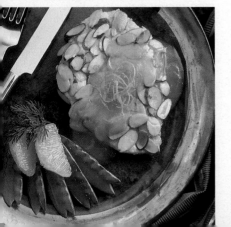

Orange Sauce

Makes ⅔ cup

> 1 tablespoon brown sugar
> 2 teaspoons cornstarch
> Juice of 1 orange (about
> ½ cup)
> 2 tablespoons butter
> 1 teaspoon grated orange
> peel

Combine brown sugar and cornstarch in saucepan. Add juice, butter and orange peel. Cook over medium heat, stirring constantly, until thickened.

Favorite recipe from **Wisconsin Milk Marketing Board** © 1993

Holiday Beef Rib Roast

Makes 10 to 12 servings

> 1 (3- to 4-rib) beef rib roast,
> well trimmed (about 6 to
> 8 pounds)

Place roast, fat side up, on rack in roasting pan. Insert meat thermometer so bulb is centered in the thickest part, not touching fat or bone. Do not add water. Do not cover. Roast in 325°F oven to desired doneness, 23 to 25 minutes per pound for rare; 27 to 30 minutes per pound for medium. Remove roast when meat thermometer registers 135°F for rare; 155°F for medium. Allow roast to stand tented with aluminum foil 15 to 20 minutes. Roast continues to rise about 5°F in temperature to reach 140°F for rare; 160°F for medium.

Favorite recipe from **National Live Stock and Meat Board**

Lamb Rib Roast Dijon

Lamb Rib Roast Dijon

Makes 2 servings

1 (6-rib) lamb rib roast (about 1¹/₂ to 1³/₄ pounds)
1 tablespoon Dijon-style mustard
¹/₃ cup soft bread crumbs
¹/₂ teaspoon dried basil leaves, crushed
Dash garlic powder
Lemon slices, if desired
Italian parsley, if desired

Trim fat from lamb rib roast; spread roast with mustard. Combine bread crumbs, basil and garlic powder; press mixture into mustard. Place roast, fat side up, on rack in shallow roasting pan. Insert meat thermometer into thickest part of roast, not touching bone or fat. Do not add water. Do not cover. Roast in 375°F oven to desired degree of doneness. Allow 30 to 35 minutes per pound for rare; 35 to 40 minutes for medium. Remove roast when meat thermometer registers 135°F for rare; 155°F for medium. Cover roast with aluminum foil tent and allow to stand 15 to 20 minutes before carving. Roast will continue to rise approximately 5°F in temperature to reach 140°F for rare; 160°F for medium. Garnish with lemon slices and Italian parsley, if desired.

Favorite recipe from **National Live Stock and Meat Board**

Breads & Muffins

Holiday Stollen

Makes 2 loaves

1½ cups (3 sticks) unsalted
    butter, softened
4 egg yolks
½ cup granulated sugar
1 teaspoon salt
    Grated peel from 1 lemon
    Grated peel from 1 orange
1 teaspoon vanilla
2½ cups hot milk (120°F–
    130°F)
8 to 8½ cups all-purpose
    flour, divided
2 packages active dry yeast
½ cup *each* golden raisins,
    candied orange peel,
    candied lemon peel,
    chopped candied red
    cherries, chopped
    candied green cherries,
    chopped almonds
1 egg, beaten
    Powdered sugar

In large mixer bowl, beat butter, egg yolks, granulated sugar, salt, lemon peel, orange peel and vanilla until light and fluffy. Slowly add milk; mix thoroughly. Add 2 cups flour and yeast; mix well. When mixture is smooth, add remaining flour, ½ cup at a time, until dough forms that can be lifted out of bowl. Lightly flour work surface; knead dough until smooth and elastic, about 10 minutes. Mix raisins, candied orange and lemon peels, cherries and almonds in medium bowl; knead fruit mixture into dough.

Place dough in greased bowl, cover with plastic wrap and let rise in warm place until doubled in bulk, about 1 hour.

Grease 2 large baking sheets. Turn dough out onto floured work surface. Divide dough in half. Place one half back into bowl; cover and set aside. Cut remaining half into thirds. Roll each third into 12-inch rope. Place on prepared baking sheet. Braid ropes together. Repeat procedure with remaining dough.

Brush beaten egg on braids. Let braids stand at room temperature until doubled in bulk, about 1 hour.

Preheat oven to 350°F. Bake braids until golden brown and sound hollow when tapped, about 45 minutes. Remove to wire rack to cool. Sprinkle with powdered sugar before serving.

Holiday Stollen

Blueberry Oat Bread

Makes 1 loaf or 12 servings

- 2 cups flour
- 1 cup uncooked quick or old-fashioned oats
- 1 tablespoon baking powder
- 1 teaspoon salt
- 1/2 teaspoon baking soda
- 1/2 teaspoon ground cinnamon
- 2 eggs
- 1 cup milk
- 1/2 cup sugar
- 1/3 cup KARO® Light Corn Syrup
- 1/4 cup MAZOLA® Corn Oil
- 1 1/2 cups fresh or frozen blueberries*

Preheat oven to 350°F. Grease and flour 9×5×3-inch loaf pan.

In large bowl, combine flour, oats, baking powder, salt, baking soda and cinnamon. In small bowl, combine eggs, milk, sugar, corn syrup and corn oil until blended; set aside. Toss blueberries in flour mixture. Stir in egg mixture until well blended. Pour batter into prepared pan.

Bake 60 to 70 minutes or until toothpick inserted in center comes out clean. Cool in pan 10 minutes. Remove from pan; cool on wire rack.

If using frozen blueberries, do not thaw before adding to flour mixture.

Irish Soda Bacon Bread

Makes 12 to 15 servings

- 4 cups all-purpose flour
- 3 tablespoons sugar
- 1 1/2 tablespoons low-sodium baking powder
- 1 teaspoon baking soda
- 6 tablespoons unsalted margarine or butter, cold
- 1 cup golden raisins
- 6 slices ARMOUR® Lower Salt Bacon, cooked crisp and crumbled
- 2 eggs
- 1 1/2 cups buttermilk

Preheat oven to 375°F. Combine flour, sugar, baking powder and baking soda in large bowl; cut in margarine until mixture resembles coarse crumbs. Stir in raisins and bacon. Beat eggs slightly in small bowl; remove and reserve 1 tablespoon egg. Add buttermilk and remaining eggs to flour mixture; stir to make soft dough. Turn out onto lightly floured surface; knead about 1 to 2 minutes or until smooth.

Shape dough into round loaf. Spray round 2-quart casserole dish with nonstick cooking spray; place dough in dish. With floured knife, cut a 4-inch "X" about 1/4 inch deep on top of loaf. Brush loaf with reserved egg. Bake about 55 to 65 minutes or until toothpick inserted into center comes out clean. (Cover loaf with foil during last 30 minutes of baking to prevent overbrowning.) Cool on wire rack 10 minutes; remove from dish. Serve with light cream cheese or honey butter, if desired.

Chocolate Cherry Cordial Muffins

Makes 12 muffins

- 2 cups all-purpose flour
- 1/4 cup granulated sugar
- 1/4 cup firmly packed brown sugar
- 2 teaspoons baking powder
- 1/2 teaspoon baking soda
- 1/2 teaspoon salt
- 2 cups (11 1/2-ounce package) NESTLÉ® Toll House® Milk Chocolate Morsels, divided
- 1/2 cup chopped candied cherries or raisins
- 3/4 cup milk
- 1/3 cup vegetable oil
- 1 egg

Preheat oven to 400°F. Grease or paper-line 12 (2 1/2-inch) muffin cups.

In large bowl, combine flour, granulated sugar, brown sugar, baking powder, baking soda and salt. Stir in 1 3/4 cups milk chocolate morsels and cherries; set aside. In small bowl, combine milk, oil and egg. Stir into flour mixture just until moistened. Spoon into prepared muffin cups (muffin cups will be full). Sprinkle with remaining 1/4 cup milk chocolate morsels.

Bake 18 to 21 minutes until golden brown. Cool 5 minutes; remove from pan.

Chocolate Cherry Cordial Muffins

Lemon Cranberry Loaves

Makes 24 slices

> 1 package DUNCAN HINES®
>   Moist Deluxe Lemon
>   Supreme Cake Mix
> 1¼ cups finely chopped fresh
>   cranberries
> ½ cup finely chopped
>   walnuts
> ¼ cup granulated sugar
> 1 package (3 ounces) cream
>   cheese, softened
> ¾ cup milk
> 4 eggs
>   Confectioners sugar

Preheat oven to 350°F. Grease and flour two 8½×4½-inch loaf pans.

Stir together cranberries, walnuts and granulated sugar in large bowl; set aside.

Combine cake mix, cream cheese and milk in large bowl. Beat at medium speed with electric mixer for 2 minutes. Add eggs, 1 at a time, beating for an additional 2 minutes. Fold in cranberry mixture. Pour into pans. Bake at 350°F for 45 to 50 minutes or until toothpick inserted in center comes out clean. Cool in pans 15 minutes. Loosen loaves from pans. Invert onto cooling rack. Turn right side up. Cool completely. Dust with confectioners sugar.

Apple Date Nut Muffins

Makes 12 muffins

> 1½ cups all-purpose flour
> ⅔ cup packed brown sugar
> ½ cup uncooked rolled oats
> 1 tablespoon baking powder
> 1 teaspoon ground cinnamon
> ½ teaspoon salt
> ⅛ teaspoon ground nutmeg
> ⅛ teaspoon ground ginger
>   Dash ground cloves
> 1 cup coarsely chopped
>   peeled apples
> ½ cup chopped walnuts
> ½ cup chopped pitted dates
> ½ cup butter or margarine,
>   melted
> ¼ cup milk
> 2 eggs

Preheat oven to 400°F. Grease well or paper-line 12 (2½-inch) muffin cups.

Combine flour, brown sugar, oats, baking powder, cinnamon, salt, nutmeg, ginger and cloves in large bowl. Mix in apples, nuts and dates. Combine butter, milk and eggs in small bowl until blended. Pour into flour mixture, stirring just until moistened. Spoon evenly into prepared muffin cups.

Bake 20 to 25 minutes or until wooden pick inserted in center comes out clean. Remove from pan.

Lemon Cranberry Loaf

Pumpkin-Ginger Scones

Pumpkin-Ginger Scones

Makes 12 scones

- ¹/₂ cup sugar, divided
- 2 cups all-purpose flour
- 2 teaspoons baking powder
- 1 teaspoon ground cinnamon
- ¹/₂ teaspoon baking soda
- ¹/₂ teaspoon salt
- 5 tablespoons butter or margarine, divided
- 1 egg
- ¹/₂ cup canned pumpkin
- ¹/₄ cup sour cream
- ¹/₂ teaspoon grated fresh ginger *or* 2 tablespoons finely chopped crystallized ginger

Preheat oven to 425°F.

Reserve 1 tablespoon sugar. Combine remaining sugar, flour, baking powder, cinnamon, baking soda and salt in large bowl. Cut in 4 tablespoons butter with pastry blender until mixture resembles coarse crumbs. Beat egg in small bowl. Add pumpkin, sour cream and ginger; beat until well combined. Add pumpkin mixture to flour mixture; stir until mixture forms soft dough that leaves side of bowl.

Turn dough out onto well-floured surface. Knead 10 times. Roll dough using floured rolling pin into 9×6-inch rectangle. Cut dough into 6 (3-inch) squares. Cut each square diagonally in half, making 12 triangles. Place triangles, 2 inches apart, on ungreased baking sheets. Melt remaining 1 tablespoon butter. Brush tops of triangles with butter and sprinkle with reserved sugar.

Bake 10 to 12 minutes or until golden brown. Cool 10 minutes on wire racks. Serve warm.

Clockwise from top: Cranberry Orange Nut Muffin, Carrot-Raisin Bran Muffin, Sweet Potato Pecan Muffin

Sweet Potato Pecan Muffins

Makes 12 muffins

> **MAZOLA® No Stick cooking spray**
1 ¾ cups flour
⅓ cup sugar
2 teaspoons baking powder
1 teaspoon ground cinnamon
½ teaspoon salt
⅛ teaspoon ground nutmeg
¾ cup cooked, mashed sweet potatoes
¾ cup **KARO® Dark Corn Syrup**
⅓ cup **MAZOLA® Corn Oil**
2 eggs
1 teaspoon vanilla
1 cup chopped pecans

Preheat oven to 400°F. Spray 12 (2½-inch) muffin pan cups with cooking spray.

In medium bowl, combine flour, sugar, baking powder, cinnamon, salt and nutmeg. In large bowl, with mixer at medium speed, beat sweet potatoes, corn syrup, corn oil, eggs and vanilla until blended. Stir in flour mixture until well blended. Stir in pecans. Spoon into prepared muffin pan cups.

Bake 20 minutes or until lightly browned and firm to the touch. Cool in pan on wire rack 5 minutes; remove from pan.

Cranberry Orange Nut Muffins

Makes 12 muffins

MAZOLA® No Stick cooking spray
1 1/2 cups flour
1/2 cup sugar
2 teaspoons baking powder
1/2 teaspoon salt
2 eggs
1/2 cup KARO® Light Corn Syrup
1/2 cup orange juice
1/4 cup MAZOLA® Corn Oil
1 teaspoon grated orange peel
1 cup fresh or frozen cranberries, chopped
1/2 cup chopped walnuts

Preheat oven to 400°F. Spray 12 (2 1/2-inch) muffin pan cups with cooking spray.

In medium bowl, combine flour, sugar, baking powder and salt. In large bowl, combine eggs, corn syrup, orange juice, corn oil and orange peel. Stir in flour mixture until well blended. Stir in cranberries and walnuts. Spoon into prepared muffin pan cups.

Bake 18 to 20 minutes or until lightly browned and firm to touch. Cool in pan on wire rack 5 minutes; remove from pan.

Carrot-Raisin Bran Muffins

Makes 12 muffins

MAZOLA® No Stick cooking spray
2 cups bran flake cereal with raisins
2/3 cup buttermilk
1/2 cup KARO® Dark Corn Syrup
1 cup flour
2 teaspoons baking soda
1 teaspoon ground cinnamon
1/4 teaspoon salt
1 egg, slightly beaten
1/4 cup sugar
1/4 cup MAZOLA® Corn Oil
1 cup shredded carrots

Preheat oven to 400°F. Spray 12 (2 1/2-inch) muffin pan cups with cooking spray.

In large bowl, mix cereal, buttermilk and corn syrup; let stand 5 minutes. In medium bowl, combine flour, baking soda, cinnamon and salt; set aside. Add egg, sugar and corn oil to cereal mixture; mix until blended. Stir in flour mixture until well blended. Stir in carrots. Spoon into prepared muffin pan cups.

Bake 20 minutes or until lightly browned and firm to touch. Cool in pan on wire rack 5 minutes; remove from pan.

Chocolate Walnut Coffee Rings

Makes 2 coffee rings

6½ to 7 cups all-purpose flour,
   divided
  ½ cup granulated sugar
1½ teaspoons salt
1½ teaspoons ground cinnamon
  2 packages active dry yeast
  1 cup (2 sticks) butter or
   margarine
  1 cup milk
  ½ cup water
  2 whole eggs
  2 egg yolks
  2 cups (12-ounce package)
   NESTLÉ® Toll House®
   Semi-Sweet Chocolate
   Morsels
  1 cup walnuts, chopped
  ⅓ cup firmly packed brown
   sugar
   Vegetable oil

GLAZE

  1 cup confectioners' sugar
  5 to 6 teaspoons milk
  ½ teaspoon vanilla extract
   Dash of ground cinnamon

In large mixer bowl, combine 2 cups flour, granulated sugar, salt, 1½ teaspoons cinnamon and yeast; set aside. In small saucepan, combine butter, 1 cup milk and water. Cook over medium heat just until very warm (120°F to 130°F), stirring occasionally. Gradually add milk mixture to flour mixture, beating until well blended. Beat in whole eggs, egg yolks and 1 cup flour. Stir in 2½ cups flour or enough to make stiff dough. Cover with waxed paper and towel; let stand at room temperature 20 minutes.

In small bowl, combine semi-sweet chocolate morsels, walnuts and brown sugar; set aside. Grease two large cookie sheets.

Sprinkle work surface with ½ cup flour. Turn dough onto surface; sprinkle dough with ½ cup flour. Knead 2 to 3 minutes until dough is smooth and elastic, adding additional flour if necessary to prevent sticking. Cut dough in half

On floured surface, roll one dough half into 16×10-inch rectangle. Sprinkle with half of walnut mixture to within ½ inch of edges. Roll up jelly-roll style beginning at long side. Moisten edge with water; pinch seam together to seal. Place seam-side down on prepared cookie sheet; shape into circle, pinching ends together to seal. With scissors or knife, cut dough at 1½-inch intervals almost to center of ring; twist ends up to expose filling. Brush with oil. Cover with plastic wrap.

Repeat with remaining dough and filling. Refrigerate 2 to 24 hours.

Preheat oven to 375°F. Remove dough from refrigerator. Carefully remove plastic wrap; let stand at room temperature 10 minutes.

Bake 25 to 30 minutes until golden brown. Cool completely on wire racks.

For Glaze, in small bowl, stir confectioners' sugar, 5 teaspoons milk, vanilla extract and dash of cinnamon until smooth. (Add additional 1 teaspoon milk if necessary for desired consistency.)

Drizzle Glaze over rings.

Chocolate Walnut Coffee Rings

For Ann

Peanut Butter Bread

Makes 1 loaf

  2 cups flour
  1/2 cup sugar
  2 teaspoons baking powder
  1/2 teaspoon baking soda
  1/2 teaspoon salt
  1 cup **SKIPPY® SUPER CHUNK®** or **CREAMY®** Peanut Butter
  1/2 cup **KARO®** Light or Dark Corn Syrup
  2 eggs
  1 cup milk

Preheat oven to 350°F. Grease and flour 9×5×3-inch loaf pan.

In medium bowl, combine flour, sugar, baking powder, baking soda and salt. In large bowl, with mixer at medium speed, beat peanut butter and corn syrup until smooth. Beat in eggs 1 at a time. Gradually beat in milk. Stir in flour mixture just until moistened. Pour into prepared pan.

Bake 50 to 55 minutes or until toothpick inserted in center comes out clean. Cool in pan 10 minutes. Remove from pan; cool on wire rack.

Left to right: Piña Colada Bread, Peanut Butter Bread, Blueberry Oat Bread (page 48)

Golden Pumpkin Twists

Makes 24 rolls

1/3 **cup butter or margarine**
1 **cup milk**
2 **packages active dry yeast**
1/2 **cup granulated sugar**
1 **teaspoon salt**
1 **cup LIBBY'S® Solid Pack
    Pumpkin**
3 **eggs, divided**
5 to 5 1/2 **cups all-purpose
    flour, divided**
1 **teaspoon water
    Poppy seeds or sesame
    seeds (optional)**

In small saucepan, melt butter. Add milk and heat to 105°F-115°F. Dissolve yeast in warm milk mixture; stir in sugar and salt. In large mixer bowl, combine yeast mixture, pumpkin, *2 eggs*, and *4 cups* flour; beat 3 minutes. Gradually mix in *1 cup* flour. On lightly floured surface, knead until smooth, working in additional flour as necessary to form stiff dough. Place dough in large, greased bowl, turning to coat all sides. Cover; let rise in warm, draft-free place for about 1 hour or until doubled. Punch dough down. Knead a few times to work out bubbles. On lightly floured surface, roll out dough into 24×10-inch rectangle. (If dough resists rolling, allow to rest 10 minutes.) Cut into 24 strips, 10 inches long and 1 inch wide. Tie each strip into a knot. Place on lightly greased cookie sheet 3 inches apart. Cover; let rise in warm, draft-free place for 30 minutes. Preheat oven to 350°F. In small bowl, beat together *remaining* egg and water. Brush on rolls; sprinkle with poppy seeds or sesame seeds, if desired. Bake 20 to 25 minutes or until golden brown. Serve warm.

Piña Colada Bread

Makes 1 loaf

2 1/2 **cups flour**
1/2 **cup sugar**
2 **teaspoons baking powder**
1/2 **teaspoon baking soda**
1/2 **teaspoon salt**
2 **eggs**
1/2 **cup KARO® Light Corn
    Syrup**
1/3 **cup MAZOLA® Corn Oil**
1/4 **cup rum**
1 **can (8 ounces) crushed
    pineapple in
    unsweetened juice,
    undrained**
1 **cup flaked coconut**

Preheat oven to 350°F. Grease and flour 9×5×3-inch loaf pan.

In medium bowl, combine flour, sugar, baking powder, baking soda and salt. In large bowl, with mixer at medium speed, beat eggs, corn syrup, corn oil and rum until blended. Gradually stir in flour mixture just until moistened. Stir in pineapple with juice and coconut. Pour into prepared pan.

Bake 60 to 65 minutes or until toothpick inserted in center comes out clean. Cool in pan 10 minutes. Remove from pan; cool on wire rack.

Cranberry Pecan Muffins

Makes 36 mini muffins

1¾ cups all-purpose flour
½ cup firmly packed light
    brown sugar
2½ teaspoons baking powder
½ teaspoon salt
¾ cup milk
¼ cup butter or margarine,
    melted
1 egg, beaten
1 cup chopped fresh
    cranberries
⅓ cup chopped pecans
1 teaspoon grated lemon
    peel

Preheat oven to 400°F. Grease or paper-line 36 (1¾-inch) mini-muffin cups.

Combine flour, brown sugar, baking powder and salt in large bowl. Combine milk, butter and egg in small bowl until blended; stir into flour mixture just until moistened. Fold in cranberries, pecans and lemon peel. Spoon into prepared muffin cups, filling almost full.

Bake 15 to 17 minutes or until wooden pick inserted in center comes out clean. Remove from pans. Cool on wire racks.

Cranberry Pecan Muffins

Apple Rolls

Makes 8 servings

Cinnamon Syrup (recipe
    follows)
2 cups unsifted all-purpose
    flour
4 teaspoons baking powder
2 teaspoons sugar
½ teaspoon salt
½ teaspoon cream of tartar
½ cup vegetable shortening
    or margarine
⅔ cup milk
4 Golden Delicious or Rome
    apples

1. Prepare Cinnamon Syrup; set aside. Generously butter 9-inch cake pan.

2. In large bowl, sift together flour, baking powder, sugar, salt and cream of tartar; cut in shortening until mixture resembles coarse crumbs. Add milk; stir with fork until dough forms a ball. Set aside. Peel and grate apples.

3. Preheat oven to 350°F. On floured surface, roll dough into ¼-inch-thick rectangle. Spread grated apples over dough; roll up jelly-roll style beginning at long side. Cut roll into 1-inch-thick slices; arrange slices, cut side down, in prepared pan. Pour Cinnamon Syrup over rolls. Bake 55 minutes or until golden brown.

Cinnamon Syrup: In medium saucepan, combine 2 cups sugar, 2 cups water, ¾ teaspoon ground cinnamon and ¼ teaspoon ground cloves. Boil 5 minutes. Remove from heat; stir in 2 tablespoons butter.

Favorite recipe from **Washington Apple Commission**

Pumpernickel Bread

Makes 3 loaves

- 1 cup (6-ounce package) NESTLÉ® Toll House® Semi-Sweet Chocolate Morsels
- 2 tablespoons butter
- 3 packages active dry yeast
- 1½ cups warm water (105°F-115°F)
- ½ cup molasses
- 3 tablespoons caraway seed, divided
- 1 tablespoon salt
- 2¾ cups rye flour
- 2½ cups all-purpose flour, divided
- Cornmeal
- 1 egg, slightly beaten
- 1 teaspoon water

Combine chocolate morsels and butter over hot (not boiling) water. Stir until morsels are melted and mixture is smooth. Set aside. In large bowl, dissolve yeast in warm water. Add molasses, 2 tablespoons caraway seed, salt, rye flour and melted morsel mixture; beat well. Stir in all-purpose flour, 1 cup at a time, to make a soft dough. Gradually add remaining ½ cup flour; mix well. Turn dough onto lightly floured board; cover with bowl. Let rest 10 minutes.

Remove bowl and knead dough until smooth and elastic (about 15 minutes). Place dough in greased bowl; turn once. Cover and let rise in warm place 1 hour. Punch dough down; cover and let rise in warm place 45 minutes. Punch dough down; divide into 3 equal parts. Shape each into a ball and place on greased cookie sheet sprinkled with cornmeal. Cover;

Pumpernickel Bread

let rise in warm place until doubled in bulk (about 1 hour). Preheat oven to 375°F. In cup, combine egg and water; brush tops of loaves with egg mixture and sprinkle with remaining 1 tablespoon caraway seed. Bake 30 to 35 minutes. Cool bread on wire racks.

Cookies & Confections

Golden Kolacky

Makes about 3 dozen cookies

    1 cup butter, softened
    4 ounces cream cheese,
      softened
    1 teaspoon vanilla
    1 cup flour
    ¹/₄ teaspoon salt
      Fruit preserves

Combine butter and cream cheese in large bowl; beat until smooth and creamy. Blend in vanilla. Combine flour and salt; gradually add to butter mixture, blending until mixture forms soft dough. Divide dough in half; wrap each half in plastic wrap. Refrigerate until firm.

Preheat oven to 375°F. Roll out dough, ¹/₂ at a time, on sugared surface to ¹/₈-inch thickness. Cut into 3-inch squares. Spoon 1 teaspoon preserves in center of each square. Bring up two opposite corners to center; pinch together tightly to seal. Fold sealed tip to one side; pinch to seal. Place 1 inch apart on ungreased cookie sheets. Bake for 10 to 15 minutes or until lightly browned. Remove to cooling racks; cool completely.

Orange Pecan Gems

Makes 4¹/₂ to 5 dozen cookies

    1 package DUNCAN HINES®
      Moist Deluxe Orange
      Supreme Cake Mix
    1 container (8 ounces)
      vanilla lowfat yogurt
    1 egg
    2 tablespoons butter or
      margarine, softened
    1 cup finely chopped pecans
    1 cup pecan halves

Preheat oven to 350°F. Grease baking sheets.

Combine cake mix, yogurt, egg, butter and chopped pecans in large bowl. Beat at low speed with electric mixer until blended. Drop by rounded teaspoonfuls 2 inches apart onto greased baking sheets. Press pecan half onto center of each cookie. Bake at 350°F for 11 to 13 minutes or until golden brown. Cool 1 minute on baking sheets. Remove to cooling racks. Cool completely. Store in airtight container.

Golden Kolacky

Left to right: Nutty Caramel Bars and Orange Creme Brownies

Nutty Caramel Bars

Makes about 24 bars

1½ cups (3 sticks) butter,
  divided
½ cup granulated sugar
1 egg
1 teaspoon vanilla
2 cups all-purpose flour
¼ cup honey
¾ cup firmly packed light
  brown sugar
¼ cup heavy (whipping)
  cream
1 can (12 ounces) lightly
  salted mixed whole nuts

Preheat oven to 350°F. Butter a 13×9-inch baking pan; set aside. In large mixer bowl, beat 1 cup (2 sticks) butter with granulated sugar until light and fluffy; beat in egg and vanilla. Stir in flour until well mixed; press evenly into prepared pan. Bake until edges are brown and center looks dry, about 15 minutes. Remove to wire rack while preparing topping. Maintain oven temperature. In heavy medium saucepan over medium heat, heat remaining ½ cup (1 stick) butter with honey until butter is melted. Stir in brown sugar; bring to a boil. Boil without stirring for exactly 2 minutes; remove from heat. Stir in cream and nuts. Immediately spoon caramel nut mixture evenly over crust. Bake until caramel bubbles, about 10 minutes. Cool completely on wire rack; cut in 2×2-inch bars. Store in tightly covered container at room temperature.

Favorite recipe from **National Dairy Board**

Orange Creme Brownies

Makes 36 bars

3/4 cup all-purpose flour
1/4 teaspoon baking powder
1/4 teaspoon salt
  1 package (6 ounces) semi-
      sweet chocolate morsels
1/2 cup (1 stick) butter, cut
      into small pieces
1/3 cup granulated sugar
  3 tablespoons orange juice
  1 teaspoon grated orange
      peel
  1 teaspoon vanilla
  2 eggs
1 1/3 cups (about 6 ounces)
      chopped walnuts
      Orange Creme (recipe
      follows)
      Chocolate Icing (recipe
      follows)

Preheat oven to 325°F. Line bottom and sides of 9-inch square baking pan with foil, allowing foil to overhang slightly. Butter foil; set aside. On square of waxed paper, combine flour, baking powder and salt. In small saucepan, combine chocolate morsels, butter, sugar and orange juice. Cook and stir over very low heat until chocolate and butter are melted; remove from heat. Stir in orange peel and vanilla. Using wire whisk, beat in eggs 1 at a time. Add reserved flour mixture, beating until smooth. Stir in nuts; spread in prepared pan. Bake until wooden pick inserted in center comes out clean, 23 to 25 minutes. Cool completely on wire rack. Spread with Orange Creme.

Refrigerate until firm, about 15 minutes, or place in freezer about 5 minutes. Spread warm Chocolate Icing over Orange Creme. Using knife, score Chocolate Icing layer in 36 (1 1/2-inch) squares; refrigerate until Chocolate Icing is firm, about 25 minutes, or place in freezer about 5 minutes. Remove from pan by lifting foil edges. Cut into squares. Refrigerate up to 4 days or wrap and freeze up to 1 month.

Orange Creme

Makes 1 1/2 cups

1/2 cup (1 stick) butter,
      softened
  2 cups confectioners sugar
  1 teaspoon grated orange
      peel
  1 teaspoon milk
  1 teaspoon vanilla

In small mixer bowl, beat butter and sugar until light and fluffy. Beat in orange peel, milk and vanilla.

Chocolate Icing

Makes about 1 cup

  1 package (6 ounces) semi-
      sweet chocolate morsels
  1 tablespoon butter
  1 tablespoon vegetable
      shortening

In small saucepan, combine chocolate morsels, butter and shortening. Stir over very low heat until melted.

Favorite recipe from **National Dairy Board**

Good Luck Meringue Mushrooms

Makes about 2¹/₂ dozen cookies

> 2 egg whites
> Pinch cream of tartar
> ¹/₂ cup sugar
> ¹/₂ cup semisweet chocolate chips, melted
> Unsweetened cocoa

Preheat oven to 250°F. Beat egg whites in small bowl until foamy. Add cream of tartar and beat until soft peaks form. Add sugar, 2 tablespoons at a time, beating until stiff and glossy. Line baking sheets with parchment paper. Spoon mixture into pastry bag fitted with large writing tip. Pipe 1-inch rounds to make mushroom caps. Smooth tops with wet fingertips. Pipe 1-inch-high cones to make stems. (Pipe an equal number of caps and cones.) Bake about 30 minutes or until firm. Turn oven off; let stand in oven 1 hour. Remove from oven; cool completely. Make small hole in center of flat side of each cap with sharp knife. Fill hole with melted chocolate. Insert stem into hole. Set aside until chocolate sets. Sift cocoa through fine sieve over mushroom caps.

Note: These can be made ahead and stored, loosely covered, at room temperature for up to 1 week. Avoid making these cookies on humid days as they may become moist and sticky.

Festive Popcorn Treats

Makes 6 servings

> 6 cups popped popcorn
> ¹/₂ cup sugar
> ¹/₂ cup light corn syrup
> ¹/₄ cup peanut butter
> Green food color
> ¹/₄ cup red cinnamon candies

Line baking sheet with waxed paper. Pour popcorn into large bowl. Combine sugar and corn syrup in medium saucepan. Bring to a boil over medium heat, stirring constantly; boil 1 minute. Remove from heat. Add peanut butter and green food color; stir until peanut butter is completely melted. Pour over popcorn; stir to coat well. Lightly butter hands and shape popcorn mixture into trees as shown in photo. While trees are still warm, press red cinnamon candies into trees. Place on prepared baking sheet; let stand until firm, about 30 minutes.

Clockwise from left:
Festive Popcorn Treats,
Good Luck Meringue Mushrooms,
Tiger Stripes (page 66)

Tiger Stripes

Makes 36 pieces

- **1 package (12 ounces) semisweet chocolate chips**
- **3 tablespoons chunky peanut butter, divided**
- **2 (2-ounce) white chocolate baking bars**

Line 8×8-inch square pan with foil. Grease lightly. Melt semisweet chocolate and 2 tablespoons peanut butter over low heat in small saucepan; stir well. Pour half of chocolate mixture into prepared pan. Let stand 10 to 15 minutes to cool slightly. Melt white baking bar with remaining 1 tablespoon peanut butter over low heat in small saucepan. Spoon half of white chocolate mixture over dark chocolate mixture. Drop remaining dark and white chocolate mixtures by spoonfuls over mixture in pan. Using small metal spatula or knife, pull through the chocolates to create tiger stripes. Freeze about 1 hour or until firm. Remove from pan; peel off foil. Cut into 36 pieces. Refrigerate until ready to serve.

Glazed Sugar Cookies

Glazed Sugar Cookies

Makes 2½ to 3 dozen cookies

COOKIES
- **1 package DUNCAN HINES® Golden Sugar Cookie Mix**
- **1 egg**

GLAZE
- **1 cup sifted confectioners sugar**
- **1 to 2 tablespoons water or milk**
- **½ teaspoon vanilla extract Food coloring (optional) Red and green sugar crystals, nonpareils or cinnamon candies**

Preheat oven to 375°F.

For Cookies, combine cookie mix, contents of buttery flavor packet from Mix and egg in large bowl. Stir until thoroughly blended. Roll dough to ⅛-inch thickness on lightly floured surface. Cut dough into desired shapes using floured cookie cutters. Place cookies 2 inches apart on ungreased baking sheets. Bake at 375°F for 5 to 6 minutes or until edges are light golden brown. Cool 1 minute on baking sheets. Remove to cooling racks. Cool completely.

For Glaze, combine confectioners sugar, water and vanilla extract in small bowl. Beat until smooth. Tint glaze with food coloring, if desired. Brush glaze on each cookie with clean pastry brush. Sprinkle cookies with sugar crystals, nonpareils or cinnamon candies before glaze sets. Allow glaze to set before storing between layers of waxed paper in airtight container.

Butter Toffee Crunch

Makes about ¾ pound

  ¾ **cup butter or margarine**
  1 **tablespoon corn syrup**
      Hot water
  1 **cup sugar**
  1 **package (2¼ ounces) sliced almonds (about ¾ cup)**

Place butter in 2-quart microwave-safe bowl. Microwave on HIGH (100% power) 1 minute or until melted.

Stir in corn syrup, 2 tablespoons hot water and sugar. Microwave on HIGH (100% power) 4 minutes, stirring after 1 minute. Add 1 tablespoon hot water; stir to combine. Microwave on HIGH (100% power) 1 minute.

Stir in almonds. Microwave on HIGH (100% power) 2 to 3 minutes, until light caramel in color.

Pour onto an ungreased baking sheet. Spread out candy. Cool until set. Break into pieces. Store in airtight container.

Variation: Sprinkle hot candy with 1 cup milk chocolate chips. Let melt; spread.

Hint: If kitchen is cold, warm baking sheet before pouring out toffee. It will spread more easily and be thinner.

German Chocolate No-Cook Fudge

German Chocolate No-Cook Fudge

Makes about 2 pounds

  3 **(4-ounce) packages German sweet chocolate, broken into pieces**
  1 **cup (6 ounces) semisweet chocolate chips**
  1 **can (14 ounces) sweetened condensed milk**
  1 **cup chopped pecans**
  2 **teaspoons vanilla**
 36 **pecan halves (optional)**

Butter 8-inch square pan; set aside.

Melt chocolate and chips in heavy, small saucepan over very low heat, stirring constantly. Remove from heat.

Stir in condensed milk, chopped pecans and vanilla until combined. Spread in prepared pan. Arrange pecan halves on fudge. Score fudge into squares with knife. Refrigerate until firm.

Cut into squares. Store in refrigerator. Bring to room temperature before serving.

Choco-Coco Pecan Crisps

Makes about 6 dozen cookies

- 1/2 cup butter or margarine, softened
- 1 cup packed light brown sugar
- 1 egg
- 1 teaspoon vanilla
- 1 1/2 cups all-purpose flour
- 1 cup chopped pecans
- 1/3 cup unsweetened cocoa
- 1/2 teaspoon baking soda
- 1 cup flaked coconut

Cream butter and sugar in large bowl until light and fluffy. Beat in egg and vanilla. Combine flour, pecans, cocoa and baking soda in small bowl until well blended. Add to creamed mixture, blending until stiff dough is formed. Sprinkle coconut on work surface. Divide dough into 4 parts. Shape each part into a roll, about 1 1/2 inches in diameter; roll in coconut until thickly coated. Wrap in plastic wrap; chill until firm, at least 1 hour or up to 2 weeks. (For longer storage, freeze up to 6 weeks.)

Preheat oven to 350°F. Cut rolls into 1/8-inch-thick slices. Place 2 inches apart on cookie sheets.

Bake 10 to 13 minutes or until firm, but not overly browned. Remove to wire racks to cool.

Holiday Fruit Drops

Makes about 8 dozen cookies

- 1/2 cup butter, softened
- 3/4 cup packed brown sugar
- 1 egg
- 1 1/4 cups all-purpose flour
- 1 teaspoon vanilla
- 1/2 teaspoon baking soda
- 1/2 teaspoon ground cinnamon
- Pinch salt
- 1 cup (8 ounces) diced candied pineapple
- 1 cup (8 ounces) red and green candied cherries
- 8 ounces chopped pitted dates
- 1 cup (6 ounces) semisweet chocolate chips
- 1/2 cup whole hazelnuts
- 1/2 cup pecan halves
- 1/2 cup coarsely chopped walnuts

Preheat oven to 325°F. Lightly grease cookie sheets or line with parchment paper. Cream butter and sugar in large bowl. Beat in egg until light. Mix in flour, vanilla, baking soda, cinnamon and salt. Stir in pineapple, cherries, dates, chocolate chips, hazelnuts, pecans and walnuts. Drop dough by rounded teaspoonfuls 2 inches apart onto prepared cookie sheets.

Bake 15 to 20 minutes or until firm and lightly browned around edges. Remove to wire racks to cool completely.

Note: The cherries, hazelnuts and pecan halves are not chopped, but left whole.

Left to right: Holiday Fruit Drops and Choco-Coco Pecan Crisps

Sugar Cookie Wreaths

Makes 2 dozen cookies

- **1 package DUNCAN HINES®
  Golden Sugar
  Cookie Mix**
- **1 egg
  Green food coloring
  Candied or maraschino
  cherry pieces**

Preheat oven to 375°F.

Combine cookie mix, buttery packet from Mix and egg in large bowl. Stir until thoroughly blended.

Tint dough with green food coloring. Stir until desired color. Form into balls the size of miniature marshmallows. For each wreath, arrange 9 or 10 balls, with sides touching, into a ring. Place wreaths 2 inches apart on ungreased baking sheets. Flatten slightly with fingers. Place small piece of candied cherry on each ball.

Bake at 375°F for 5 to 7 minutes or until set but not browned. Cool 1 minute on baking sheets. Remove to cooling racks. Cool completely. Store in airtight container.

Sugar Cookie Wreaths

Cranberry Almond Squares

Makes 24 servings

- **3 cups cranberries**
- **1 cup raisins**
- **1 cup peeled, chopped apple**
- **1 cup unsweetened apple
  juice**
- **1 tablespoon granulated
  sugar**
- **1½ cups whole-wheat flour**
- **1 cup regular oats, uncooked**
- **⅓ cup firmly packed brown
  sugar**
- **1 teaspoon ground cinnamon**
- **⅛ teaspoon salt**
- **½ cup molasses**
- **¼ cup CRISCO® Oil**
- **2 tablespoons slivered
  almonds, toasted,
  chopped**

Heat oven to 350°F. Lightly oil 13×9-inch pan. Combine cranberries, raisins, apple, apple juice and granulated sugar in saucepan. Bring to a boil. Cook 5 minutes or until cranberry skins pop, stirring occasionally. Reduce heat and simmer, uncovered, 10 minutes. Stir occasionally. Cool.

Combine flour, oats, brown sugar, cinnamon and salt in a medium bowl. Combine molasses and Crisco® Oil; add to flour mixture. Toss with fork until mixture resembles coarse meal.

Press 2 cups flour mixture in bottom of prepared pan. Top with cranberry mixture. Spread evenly. Combine remaining flour mixture and almonds. Sprinkle over cranberry mixture. Press lightly.

Bake at 350°F for 35 minutes or until golden. Cool. Cut into squares. Store loosely covered.

Left to right: Eggnog Gift Fudge and Cherry Merry Christmas Crunch

Eggnog Gift Fudge

Makes 36 pieces

    3/4 cup prepared eggnog
      2 tablespoons light corn
        syrup
      2 tablespoons butter or
        margarine
      2 cups sugar
      1 teaspoon vanilla

Butter 8×8-inch pan. Lightly
butter inside of heavy, medium
saucepan. Combine eggnog, corn
syrup, butter and sugar in
prepared saucepan. Cook over
medium heat, stirring constantly,
until sugar dissolves and mixture
comes to a boil. Wash down side
of pan with pastry brush
frequently dipped in hot water to
remove sugar crystals. Add candy
thermometer. Continue to cook
until mixture reaches 238°F (soft-
ball stage). Pour into large
heatproof bowl. Cool to lukewarm
(about 110°F). Add vanilla; beat
with heavy-duty electric mixer
until thick. Spread in prepared
pan. Score fudge into 36 squares.
Refrigerate until firm. Cut into
squares. Wrap in plastic wrap and
top with bows as shown in photo.

Cherry Merry Christmas Crunch

Makes about 2 pounds candy

      2 cups walnut halves
      1 cup candied red and green
        cherries, cut in half
      2 tablespoons butter or
        margarine
      1 teaspoon maple extract
    1/4 teaspoon cherry extract
      1 teaspoon salt
      2 cups sugar
    3/4 cup light corn syrup
    1/4 cup maple syrup

Generously grease baking sheet.

Combine walnuts, cherries, butter,
extracts and salt in medium bowl;
set aside. Combine sugar, corn
syrup and maple syrup in heavy,
large saucepan. Bring to a boil.
Cook over medium heat until
mixture reaches 300°F on candy
thermometer (hard-crack stage).
Remove from heat; stir in walnut
mixture. Quickly pour onto
prepared pan. Cool completely.
Break into pieces.

Star Christmas Tree Cookies

Makes 2 to 3 dozen cookies

COOKIES
- 1/2 cup CRISCO® Shortening
- 1/3 cup butter or margarine, softened
- 2 egg yolks
- 1 teaspoon vanilla extract
- 1 package DUNCAN HINES® Moist Deluxe Yellow or Devil's Food Cake Mix
- 1 tablespoon water

FROSTING
- 1 container (16 ounces) DUNCAN HINES® Creamy Homestyle Vanilla Frosting
- Green food coloring
- Red and green sugar crystals for garnish
- Assorted colored candies and decors for garnish

Preheat oven to 375°F. For Cookies, combine shortening, butter, egg yolks and vanilla extract. Blend in cake mix gradually. Add 1 teaspoonful water at a time until dough is rolling consistency. Divide dough into 4 balls. Flatten one ball with hand; roll to 1/8-inch thickness on lightly floured surface. Cut with graduated star cookie cutters. Repeat using remaining dough. Bake large cookies together on ungreased baking sheet. Bake 6 to 8 minutes or until edges are light golden brown. Cool cookies 1 minute. Remove from baking sheet. Repeat with smaller cookies, testing for doneness at minimum baking time.

For Frosting, tint vanilla frosting with green food coloring. Frost cookies and stack beginning with largest cookies on bottom and ending with smallest cookies on top. Rotate cookies when stacking to alternate corners. Decorate as desired with colored sugar crystals and assorted colored candies and decors.

Almond-Coconut Balls

Makes about 24 balls

- 1 can (7 ounces) almond paste
- 1/3 cup powdered sugar
- 1 cup flaked coconut
- 1 to 2 teaspoons water
- 7 ounces pastel-colored confectioner's coating

Line baking sheet with buttered waxed paper; set aside.

Combine almond paste, sugar and coconut in medium bowl. Stir in water if mixture is dry.

For each candy, shape 1 scant tablespoonful of mixture into 1-inch ball. Place balls on prepared baking sheet. Refrigerate until set, about 30 minutes.

Melt confectioner's coating in bowl over hot, not boiling water, stirring constantly.

Dip balls in coating to cover. Remove excess coating by scraping bottom of ball across rim of saucepan. Return to baking sheet. Reheat coating if it gets too thick. Refrigerate until set, about 30 minutes.

Star Christmas Tree Cookies

Peanut Butter Reindeer

Peanut Butter Reindeer

Makes about 2 dozen cookies

COOKIES
- 1 package DUNCAN HINES®
  Peanut Butter
  Cookie Mix
- 1 egg
- 2 teaspoons all-purpose
  flour

ASSORTED DECORATIONS
  Miniature semi-sweet
  chocolate chips
  Vanilla milk chips
  Candy-coated semi-sweet
  chocolate chips
  Colored sprinkles

For Cookies, combine cookie mix, contents of peanut butter packet from Mix and egg in large bowl. Stir until thoroughly blended. Form dough into ball. Place flour in jumbo (15×13-inch) resealable plastic bag. Place ball of dough in bag. Shake to coat with flour.

Place dough in center of bag (do not seal). Roll dough with rolling pin out to edges of bag. Slide bag onto baking sheet. Chill in refrigerator at least 1 hour.

Preheat oven to 375°F.

Use scissors to cut bag down center and across ends. Turn plastic back to uncover dough. Dip reindeer cookie cutter in flour. Cut dough with reindeer cookie cutter. Dip cookie cutter in flour after each cut. Transfer cutout cookies, using floured pancake turner, to ungreased baking sheets. Decorate as desired, making eyes, mouth, nose and tail with assorted decorations. Bake at 375°F for 5 to 7 minutes or until set but not browned. Cool 2 minutes on baking sheets. Remove to cooling racks. Cool completely. Store between layers of waxed paper in airtight container.

Sugared Nuts

Makes about 1 pound

- 1 cup sugar
- 1/2 cup water
- 2 1/2 cups unsalted mixed nuts
- 1 teaspoon vanilla

Grease baking sheet; set aside.

Combine sugar and water in medium saucepan. Cook, stirring constantly, over medium heat until sugar dissolves.

Add and vanilla. Cook, stirring occasionally, until water evaporates and nuts are sugary, about 12 minutes.

Spread on prepared baking sheet, separating nuts. Let stand until cooled.

Caramel Lace Chocolate Chip Cookies

Makes about 3 dozen cookies

- **¼ cup BUTTER FLAVOR CRISCO®**
- **½ cup light corn syrup**
- **1 tablespoon brown sugar**
- **½ teaspoon vanilla**
- **1½ teaspoons grated orange peel (optional)**
- **½ cup all-purpose flour**
- **¼ teaspoon salt**
- **⅓ cup semi-sweet chocolate chips**
- **⅓ cup coarsely chopped pecans**

Preheat oven to 375°F. Grease baking sheet with Butter Flavor Crisco®

Combine Butter Flavor Crisco®, corn syrup, brown sugar, vanilla and orange peel in large bowl. Beat at medium speed of electric mixer until well blended.

Combine flour and salt. Mix into creamed mixture at low speed until blended. Stir in chocolate chips and pecans. Drop teaspoonfuls of dough 4 inches apart onto baking sheet.

Bake 5 minutes or until edges are golden brown. (Chips and nuts will remain in center while dough spreads out.) *Do not overbake.* Cool 2 minutes on baking sheet. Lift cookie edge with edge of spatula. Grasp cookie edge gently and lightly pinch or flute the edge, bringing it up to the chips and pecans in center. Work around each cookie until completely fluted. Remove to cooling rack.

Caramel Lace Chocolate Chip Cookies

Double Chocolate-Creme Fudge

Makes about 4 pounds

- 1 can (12 ounces) evaporate milk
- 2 cups (11½ ounces) milk chocolate chips
- 1 cup (6 ounces) semisweet chocolate chips
- 1 jar (7 ounces) marshmallow creme
- ¼ cup butter or margarine
- 4 cups sugar
  Dash salt
- 1 teaspoon vanilla
- 2½ to 3 cups chopped pecans, divided

Butter 13×9-inch pan; set aside. Lightly butter side of heavy, large saucepan.

Combine evaporated milk, chips, marshmallow creme, butter, sugar and salt in prepared saucepan. Cook over medium heat, stirring constantly, until sugar dissolves and mixture comes to a boil. Wash down side of pan with pastry brush frequently dipped in hot water to remove sugar crystals.

Add candy thermometer. Stir mixture occasionally. Continue to cook until mixture reaches the soft-ball stage (238°F). Pour into large heatproof mixer bowl. Cool to lukewarm. Add vanilla and beat with heavy-duty electric mixer until thick. Beat in 1 cup chopped pecans when candy starts to lose its gloss. Immediately spread in prepared pan. Sprinkle remaining chopped pecans over fudge; gently press into fudge. Score fudge into squares. Refrigerate until firm.

Cut into squares. Refrigerate.

Sour Cream Fudge

Makes about 1¼ pounds

- ¾ cup sour cream
- ¼ cup milk
- 2 tablespoons corn syrup
- 2 tablespoons butter or margarine
- 2 cups sugar
- 1 teaspoon vanilla
- ½ cup walnut halves (optional)

Butter 8-inch square pan; set aside. Lightly butter side of heavy, medium saucepan.

Combine sour cream, milk, corn syrup, butter and sugar in prepared saucepan. Cook over medium heat, stirring constantly, until sugar dissolves and mixture comes to a boil. Wash down side of pan with pastry brush frequently dipped in hot water to remove sugar crystals.

Add candy thermometer. Continue to cook until mixture reaches soft-ball stage (238°F).

Pour into large heatproof mixer bowl. Cool to lukewarm (about 110°F).

Add vanilla and beat with heavy-duty electric mixer until thick. Spread into prepared pan. Score fudge into small squares. Refrigerate until firm.

Cut into squares. Place walnut half on each piece. Refrigerate.

Top to bottom: Double Chocolate-Creme Fudge and Sour Cream Fudge

Pecan Date Bars

Makes 32 bars

CRUST
1/3 cup cold butter or
    margarine
1 package DUNCAN HINES®
    Moist Deluxe White
    Cake Mix
1 egg

TOPPING
1 package (8 ounces)
    chopped dates
1 1/4 cups chopped pecans
1 cup water
1/2 teaspoon vanilla extract
    Confectioners' sugar

Preheat oven to 350°F. Grease and
flour 13×9-inch pan.

For Crust, cut butter into cake mix
with a pastry blender or 2 knives
until mixture is crumbly. Add egg;
stir well (mixture will be crumbly).
Pat mixture into bottom of pan.

For Topping, combine dates,
pecans and water in medium
saucepan. Bring to a boil. Reduce
heat and simmer until mixture

thickens, stirring constantly.
Remove from heat. Stir in vanilla
extract. Spread date mixture
evenly over crust. Bake 25 to 30
minutes. Cool completely in pan
on wire rack. Dust with
confectioners' sugar.

Milk Chocolate Orange Truffles

Makes about 6 dozen

2 cups (11 1/2-ounce package)
    NESTLÉ® Toll House®
    Milk Chocolate Morsels
1 cup (6-ounce package)
    NESTLÉ® Toll House®
    Semi-Sweet Chocolate
    Morsels
3/4 cup heavy or whipping
    cream
1 teaspoon grated orange
    rind
2 tablespoons orange-
    flavored liqueur
1 1/2 cups toasted walnuts,
    finely chopped

Line three large cookie sheets with
waxed paper. Place milk chocolate
morsels and semi-sweet chocolate
morsels in large bowl; set aside. In
small saucepan over low heat,
bring heavy cream and orange
rind just to a boil; pour over
morsels. Let stand 1 minute; whisk
until smooth. Whisk in liqueur.
Transfer to small mixer bowl; press
plastic wrap directly on surface.
Refrigerate 35 to 45 minutes, *just*
until mixture begins to thicken.
Beat 10 to 15 seconds, *just* until
chocolate mixture has lightened in
color. *(Do not overbeat or truffles
will be grainy.)* Shape rounded
teaspoonfuls of chocolate mixture

Pecan Date Bars

into balls; place on prepared cookie sheets. Refrigerate 10 to 15 minutes. Roll in walnuts. Refrigerate in airtight containers.

Chocolate-Coated Truffles:
Omit walnuts. Line three large cookie sheets with foil. Prepare chocolate mixture and shape into balls as directed. Freeze 30 to 40 minutes until firm. Melt an additional 2 cups (11½-ounce package) Nestlé® Toll House® Milk Chocolate Morsels with 3 tablespoons vegetable shortening. Drop frozen truffles, one at a time, into chocolate mixture. Stir quickly and gently to coat; remove with fork, shaking off excess coating. Return to cookie sheets. Refrigerate 10 to 15 minutes until firm. Refrigerate in airtight containers.

Sour Cream Mint Chocolate Cookies

Sour Cream Mint Chocolate Cookies

Makes about 8 dozen cookies

- 1 cup (2 sticks) butter, softened
- 2 cups granulated sugar
- 2 eggs
- 1 cup melted semisweet chocolate chips
- 1 cup sour cream
- 1½ teaspoons vanilla
- 2 teaspoons baking soda
- 1 teaspoon baking powder
- 4 cups all-purpose flour
  Creamy Mint Frosting (recipe follows)
- ½ cup crushed candy canes

Preheat oven to 350°F. In large mixer bowl, cream butter and granulated sugar until light and fluffy. Add eggs, 1 at a time, beating well after each addition. Add chocolate, sour cream and vanilla; mix well. Combine dry ingredients in large bowl; mix well. Add dry ingredients to chocolate mixture; mix until thoroughly combined. Drop rounded teaspoonfuls of dough 2 inches apart onto cookie sheets. Bake 10 to 12 minutes or until top of cookie springs back when touched lightly. Remove cookies to cooling racks; cool completely. Frost with Creamy Mint Frosting; sprinkle with crushed candy canes.

Creamy Mint Frosting

Makes 3 cups frosting

- 1 cup (2 sticks) butter, softened
- 4 cups powdered sugar
- 1 tablespoon milk
- 1 teaspoon vanilla
- ½ teaspoon mint extract

In small mixer bowl, mix butter, powdered sugar, milk, vanilla and mint extract until fluffy.

Desserts

Easy Chocolate Berry Charlotte

Makes 8 to 10 servings

CAKE
- 1/2 cup all-purpose flour
- 1/4 teaspoon baking powder
- 1/4 teaspoon salt
- 3 eggs
- 1/2 cup granulated sugar
- 1 teaspoon vanilla extract
- 2 tablespoons vegetable oil
  Confectioners' sugar
- 1 cup strawberry jam

FILLING
- 3 foil-wrapped bars
  (6 ounces) NESTLÉ®
  Semi-Sweet Chocolate
  Baking Bars
- 1 cup heavy or whipping
  cream
- 4 to 6 cups strawberry ice
  cream, softened
  Whipped cream for
  garnish
  Strawberries for garnish

For Cake, preheat oven to 350°F. Grease 15 1/2×10 1/2×1-inch baking pan. Line bottom with waxed paper. In small bowl, combine flour, baking powder and salt; set aside. In large mixer bowl, beat eggs, granulated sugar and vanilla extract until thick and pale yellow. Beat in oil and flour mixture. Spread in prepared pan.

Bake 13 to 16 minutes until golden brown. Sprinkle cloth towel with confectioners' sugar. Immediately invert cake onto towel. Gently peel off waxed paper. Starting at long side, roll warm cake jelly-roll style with towel inside. Place seam-side down on wire rack; cool. Unroll cake. Spread jam over cake to within 1/2 inch of edges; roll up cake. Wrap tightly in foil; freeze 2 hours.

For Filling, in small saucepan over low heat, melt semi-sweet chocolate baking bars with heavy cream, stirring until smooth. Remove from heat; cool completely.

Slice jelly roll into 1/2-inch slices. Tightly line bottom and sides of 2 1/2-quart bowl or 6-cup charlotte mold with cake slices. Spoon 1/3 of ice cream into lined mold. Spread half of Filling over ice cream. Repeat layers; top with remaining ice cream. Cover with plastic wrap; freeze until firm or up to 1 week. To serve, remove plastic wrap; dip mold into bowl of warm water for 15 to 20 seconds. Invert mold onto serving platter; remove mold. Let stand at room temperature 15 minutes until slightly softened. Garnish with whipped cream and strawberries.

Easy Chocolate Berry Charlotte

Nutty Golden Apple Dumplings

Makes 4 servings

1¹/₃ cups flour
1¹/₄ teaspoons baking powder
¹/₄ teaspoon salt
¹/₃ cup shortening
¹/₂ cup milk
¹/₄ cup *each* raisins, chopped
    nuts
1 tablespoon packed brown
    sugar
1 tablespoon melted butter
    or margarine
4 Golden Delicious apples,
    pared and cored
1 egg, beaten
1 tablespoon water
    Hot Cinnamon Sauce
    (recipe follows)

Preheat oven to 375°F. Combine flour, baking powder and salt; cut in shortening until mixture is consistency of cornmeal. Add milk; mix until soft dough is formed. (Dough will be slightly sticky.) Roll dough into 12-inch square on floured board. Cut into 4 (6×6-inch) squares. Combine raisins, nuts, sugar and butter. Stuff centers of apples with raisin mixture. Place apple in center of each pastry square. Moisten edges of dough with water and bring corners up over apples; seal edges. Brush with beaten egg mixture. Bake 40 minutes or until apples are tender. Serve with Hot Cinnamon Sauce.

Hot Cinnamon Sauce: Mix together ¹/₄ cup sugar and 3 tablespoons flour. Add 1 cup water and 3 tablespoons lemon juice; cook until thickened. Add 1 tablespoon butter or margarine, ¹/₂ teaspoon ground cinnamon and ¹/₄ teaspoon ground nutmeg.
Makes 1¹/₂ cups.

Favorite recipe from **Washington Apple Commission**

Kahlúa® Black Forest Cake

Makes 1 (9-inch) cake

1 package (18.25 ounces)
    chocolate fudge cake
    mix with pudding
3 eggs
³/₄ cup water
¹/₂ cup KAHLÚA®
¹/₃ cup vegetable oil
1 can (16 ounces) vanilla or
    chocolate frosting
1 can (21 ounces) cherry
    filling and topping
    Chocolate sprinkles or
    chocolate shavings for
    garnish (optional)

Preheat oven to 350°F. Grease and flour 2 (9-inch) cake pans; set aside. In large mixer bowl, prepare cake mix according to package directions, using eggs, water, Kahlúa® and oil. Pour batter into prepared pans. Bake 25 to 35 minutes, or until toothpick

Nutty Golden Apple Dumplings

Kablúa® Black Forest Cake

inserted in center comes out clean. Cool cake in pans 10 minutes; turn layers out onto racks to cool completely.

Place one cake layer bottom-side up on serving plate. Spread thick layer of canned frosting in a circle, 1½ inches around outer edge of cake. Spoon half of cherry filling into center of cake layer to frosting edge. Top with second cake layer, bottom-side down. Repeat with frosting and remaining cherry filling. Spread remaining frosting around side of cake. Decorate with chocolate sprinkles or shavings, if desired.

Maple Mousse

Makes 8 servings

  2 cups whipping cream
  1 envelope unflavored
     gelatin
  1/4 cup cold water
  4 eggs,* separated
  1 cup pure maple syrup
  1/8 teaspoon cream of tartar
  1/4 cup sugar
  1/2 teaspoon vanilla extract
    Chopped pecans, if desired

In large mixer bowl, whip cream until soft peaks form; refrigerate. Sprinkle gelatin over water to soften. Beat egg yolks in small mixer bowl until lemon colored, about 2 minutes. Gradually beat in maple syrup. Transfer egg yolk mixture to medium heavy saucepan. Stir in gelatin mixture. Heat over medium heat, stirring constantly, until gelatin is dissolved. Remove from heat. Pour into large bowl. Refrigerate until slightly thickened. Combine egg whites and cream of tartar. Beat until foamy. Gradually beat in sugar until stiff and glossy. Fold egg whites, whipped cream and vanilla into maple mixture. Divide mixture evenly between 8 fluted champagne glasses. Refrigerate 2 to 3 hours or until firm. Garnish each serving with chopped nuts.

Favorite recipe from **American Dairy Industry Association**

Use only grade A, clean uncracked eggs.

Dried Fruit and Noodle Dessert

Makes 10 to 12 servings

  8 ounces dried medium-wide
    egg noodles
  1 (8-ounce) package cream
    cheese, softened
  1 cup dairy sour cream
  6 tablespoons butter,
    softened
  1/3 cup sugar
  3 tablespoons honey
  1 teaspoon vanilla extract
  5 eggs
  2 (6-ounce) packages diced
    dried mixed fruit
  1 tablespoon sugar
  1/2 teaspoon cinnamon

Preheat oven to 350°F. Cook noodles according to package directions; rinse, drain and set aside. Meanwhile, beat cream cheese in small mixer bowl until smooth and fluffy. Beat in sour cream, butter, 1/3 cup sugar, honey and vanilla until well blended. Beat in eggs. Combine noodles and dried fruit in large mixing bowl. Stir in cream cheese mixture until all ingredients are well combined. Pour into well-buttered 2-quart casserole. Combine 1 tablespoon sugar and cinnamon. Sprinkle over top of noodle mixture. Bake 1 hour or until knife inserted near center comes out clean. Cool on wire rack. Serve warm or at room temperature.

Favorite recipe from **American Dairy Industry Association**

*Top to bottom: Maple Mousse,
Dried Fruit and Noodle Dessert*

Pink Peppermint Surprise

Makes 12 to 16 servings

- 1 package DUNCAN HINES® Angel Food Cake Mix
- 1 teaspoon peppermint extract
- 6 to 8 drops red food coloring
- ½ gallon vanilla ice cream
- ½ cup chocolate fudge ice cream topping
- Peppermint candies, crushed

Preheat oven to 375°F.

For cake, add peppermint extract and 6 to 8 drops food coloring to egg white packet and water. Prepare, bake and cool cake following package directions.

Serve each cake slice with vanilla ice cream, chocolate fudge ice cream topping and crushed peppermint candy.

Pink Peppermint Surprise

Golden Apple-Mincemeat Cake

Makes 16 servings

- 3 cups flour
- 4 teaspoons baking powder
- 1 teaspoon *each* ground allspice, cinnamon
- ½ teaspoon salt
- 1½ cups vegetable oil
- 1½ cups packed brown sugar
- 2 cups grated Golden Delicious apples
- 1 cup prepared mincemeat
- ½ cup chopped pecans
- 1½ teaspoons vanilla
- 3 eggs
- 1 to 2 tablespoons powdered sugar
- Hard Sauce (recipe follows)

Preheat oven to 350°F. Combine flour, baking powder, allspice, cinnamon and salt in large bowl; set aside. In large bowl of electric mixer, combine oil and brown sugar; beat well. Add half the flour mixture; mix well. Blend in grated apple, mincemeat, pecans and vanilla. Add remaining flour mixture. Add eggs, 1 at a time; beat well after each addition. Turn into greased 10-inch bundt pan. Bake 1 hour or until toothpick inserted near center comes out clean. Cool in pan 15 minutes; turn out onto wire rack. When cool, dust with powdered sugar. If desired, cake can be served slightly warm with Hard Sauce.

Hard Sauce: Beat ½ cup margarine and ⅛ teaspoon salt until light. Gradually beat in 1 cup powdered sugar. Stir in 1 tablespoon brandy. Refrigerate 1 hour.

Favorite recipe from **Washington Apple Commission**

Snowman Cupcakes

Snowman Cupcakes

Makes 15 snowmen

> 1 package (18.5 ounces)
>   yellow or white cake
>   mix, plus ingredients to
>   prepare mix
> 2 (16-ounce) containers
>   vanilla frosting
> 4 cups flaked coconut
> 15 large marshmallows
> 15 miniature chocolate
>   covered peanut butter
>   cups, unwrapped
>   Decorations: Small red
>   candies and pretzel
>   sticks
>   Green and red decorating
>   gel

Preheat oven to 350°F. Line 15
regular-size (2½-inch) muffin pan
cups and 15 small (about 1-inch)
muffin pan cups with paper
muffin cups. Prepare cake mix
according to package directions.
Spoon batter into muffin cups.

Bake 10 to 15 minutes for small
cupcakes and 15 to 20 minutes for
large cupcakes or until cupcakes
are golden and wooden toothpick
inserted into centers comes out
clean. Cool in pans on wire rack
10 minutes. Remove from pans to
racks; cool completely. Remove
paper liners.

For each snowman, frost bottom
and side of 1 large cupcake; coat
with coconut. Repeat with 1 small
cupcake. Attach small cupcake to
large cupcake with frosting to
form snowman body. Attach
marshmallow to small cupcake
with frosting to form snowman
head. Attach inverted peanut
butter cup to marshmallow with
frosting to form snowman hat. Use
pretzels for arms and small red
candies for buttons as shown in
photo. Pipe faces with decorating
gel as shown. Repeat with
remaining cupcakes.

Date-Nut Pumpkin Pie

Makes 1 (9-inch) pie

CRUST
    9-inch Classic Crisco®
    Single Crust (recipe
    follows)

DATE-NUT LAYER
 1 package (8 ounces) pitted
    whole dates, chopped
 ³/₄ cup water
 ¹/₃ cup firmly packed brown
    sugar
 ¹/₄ cup butter or margarine
 ¹/₂ cup chopped walnuts
 ¹/₂ teaspoon cinnamon

FILLING
 2 eggs
 1¹/₂ cups mashed, cooked or
    canned solid-pack
    pumpkin (not pumpkin
    pie filling)
 ¹/₂ cup granulated sugar
 ¹/₂ cup firmly packed brown
    sugar
 1 cup evaporated milk
 ¹/₂ teaspoon cinnamon
 ¹/₂ teaspoon ginger
 ¹/₂ teaspoon nutmeg
 ¹/₄ teaspoon salt
 ¹/₈ teaspoon cloves

GARNISH
    Sweetened whipped cream

For Crust, prepare Classic Crisco®
Single Crust. Do not bake. Reserve
dough scraps for cutouts, if
desired.* Heat oven to 450°F.

For Date-Nut Layer, combine dates
and water in medium saucepan.
Cook on medium heat until
mixture comes to a boil and dates
have softened. Add ¹/₃ cup brown
sugar and butter. Stir to blend.
Remove from heat. Stir in nuts and
cinnamon. Cool while preparing
filling.

For Filling, beat eggs lightly in
medium bowl. Add pumpkin,
granulated sugar, ¹/₂ cup brown
sugar, evaporated milk, cinnamon,
ginger, nutmeg, salt and cloves.
Stir to blend.

Spoon date-nut mixture into
unbaked pie crust. Pour in Filling.
Bake at 450°F for 10 minutes.
*Reduce oven temperature to
350°F.* Bake 35 minutes or until
knife inserted in center comes out
clean. Cool to room temperature
before serving.

For Garnish, spoon whipped
cream around outer edge of pie
just before serving. Refrigerate
leftover pie.

**Flute edge or cut small leaves
and pumpkins from pastry scraps
and press around edge of
unbaked pie crust.*

Classic Crisco® Single Crust

Makes 8- to 9-inch single crust

 1¹/₃ cups all-purpose flour
 ¹/₂ teaspoon salt
 ¹/₂ cup CRISCO® Shortening
 3 tablespoons cold water

Date-Nut Pumpkin Pie

Spoon flour into measuring cup and level. Combine flour and salt in medium bowl.

Cut in Crisco® using pastry blender (or 2 knives) until all flour is blended to form pea-size chunks.

Sprinkle with water, 1 tablespoon at a time. Toss lightly with fork until dough forms a ball.

Press dough between hands to form a 5- to 6-inch "pancake." Flour rolling surface and rolling pin lightly. Roll dough into circle.

Trim 1 inch larger than upside-down pie plate. Loosen dough carefully.

Fold dough into quarters. Unfold and press into pie plate. Fold edge under. Flute.

Orange-Filled Cream Puffs

Orange-Filled Cream Puffs

Makes 6 servings

- 3/4 cup granulated sugar
- 3 tablespoons cornstarch
- 1 1/2 cups orange juice
- 3 egg yolks, beaten
- 1 cup DANNON® Plain or Vanilla Lowfat Yogurt
- 2 tablespoons margarine or butter
- 6 Cream Puffs (recipe follows)
- 1 can (11 ounces) mandarin orange sections, drained
- Confectioner's sugar

In medium saucepan, combine granulated sugar, cornstarch and orange juice. Cook and stir over medium heat until bubbly; cook and stir 2 minutes more. Remove from heat. Gradually stir half of hot mixture into egg yolks. Return to saucepan. Bring to a boil. Reduce heat. Cook and stir 2 minutes more. Remove from heat. Stir in yogurt and margarine. Cover; chill 4 hours.

To serve, spoon filling into bottoms of cream puffs. Pile orange sections on top of filling. Add cream puff tops. Lightly sift confectioner's sugar over tops.

Cream Puffs: Preheat oven to 400°F. Grease baking sheet. In medium saucepan, combine 1 cup water and 1/2 cup margarine. Bring to a boil, stirring until margarine melts. Add 1 cup all-purpose flour and 1/2 teaspoon salt all at once, stirring vigorously. Cook and stir until mixture forms a ball that does not separate. Remove from heat and cool 10 minutes. Add 4 eggs, 1 at a time, beating after each addition until mixture is smooth.

Drop heaping tablespoons of batter into 10 mounds, 3 inches apart, onto prepared baking sheet. Bake about 35 minutes or until golden brown and puffy. Cool slightly. Cut off tops and remove any soft dough inside. Cool completely on wire rack. Freeze remaining cream puffs.

Makes 10 cream puffs.

Holiday Oreo® Peppermint Ice Cream Cake

Makes 10 to 12 servings

**1/2 gallon peppermint stick ice cream,* slightly softened
1 (7-ounce) package Mini OREO® Bite Size Chocolate Sandwich Cookies
13 peppermint candy sticks, broken into 2-inch pieces or 20 small candy canes
Whipped cream and green colored sugar, for garnish**

In 9-inch springform pan or in plastic wrap lined 9-inch cake pan, evenly spread half the ice cream. Insert 2 cookies vertically stacked, end to end, into ice cream layer against side of pan. Alternately insert candy sticks and stacked cookies around edge of pan. Reserve 8 cookies for garnish; arrange remaining cookies over ice cream layer. Spread remaining ice cream over cookie layer. Wrap and freeze until firm, at least 4 hours.

To serve, remove cake from pan to serving plate; garnish with whipped cream, reserved cookies and colored sugar if desired.

Easy Peppermint Stick Ice Cream: In large bowl, fold 1/2 cup crushed peppermint candies, 1/2 teaspoon peppermint extract and 3 drops red food coloring into 1/2 gallon vanilla ice cream, slightly softened.

Country Holiday Crisp

Makes 8 servings

**6 cups apples, pared and sliced
1/4 cup orange juice
2 cups RALSTON® brand Fruit Muesli with Cranberries
1/2 cup all-purpose flour
1/3 cup sugar
1/4 cup (1/2 stick) margarine or butter, softened
1 teaspoon ground cinnamon
Vanilla ice cream (optional)**

Preheat oven to 375°F. In ungreased 2-quart baking dish, place apples and orange juice; toss lightly. In medium bowl, place cereal, flour, sugar, margarine and cinnamon; blend together. Sprinkle cereal mixture over apples. Bake, covered, 30 to 35 minutes or until apples are tender. Uncover and bake an additional 10 minutes. Serve with vanilla ice cream if desired.

Microwave Directions: In ungreased 2-quart microwave-safe baking dish, place apples and orange juice; toss lightly. In medium bowl, place cereal, flour, sugar, margarine and cinnamon; blend together. Sprinkle cereal mixture over apples. Microwave on HIGH (100% power) 10 to 12 minutes or until apples are tender. Serve with vanilla ice cream if desired.

Acknowledgments

The publishers would like to thank the companies and organizations listed below for the use of their recipes in this publication.

American Dairy Industry
  Association
Armour Swift-Eckrich
Best Foods, a Division of CPC
  International, Inc.
Borden Kitchens, Borden, Inc.
Checkerboard Kitchens,
  Ralston Purina Company
The Dannon Company, Inc.
Delmarva Poultry Industry, Inc.
Del Monte Foods
Dole Food Company, Inc.
The HVR Company
Kahlúa Liqueur
Thomas J. Lipton Co.
Michigan Apple Committee

Nabisco Foods Group
National Dairy Board
National Fisheries Institute
National Live Stock and Meat Board
National Pasta Association
National Pork Producers Council
National Turkey Federation
Nestlé Food Company
Pollio Dairy Products
The Procter & Gamble Company
Reckitt & Colman Inc.
Riviana Foods Inc.
USA Rice Council
Washington Apple Commission
Wisconsin Milk Marketing Board

Photo Credits

The publishers would like to thank the companies and organizations listed below for the use of their photographs in this publication.

American Dairy Industry
  Association
Best Foods, a Division of CPC
  International, Inc.
Borden Kitchens, Borden, Inc.
The Dannon Company, Inc.
Del Monte Foods
The HVR Company
Kahlúa Liqueur
National Dairy Board
National Fisheries Institute

National Live Stock and Meat Board
National Pork Producers Council
National Turkey Federation
Nestlé Food Company
The Procter & Gamble Company
Reckitt & Colman Inc.
Riviana Foods Inc.
USA Rice Council
Washington Apple Commission
Wisconsin Milk Marketing Board

Index

METRIC CONVERSION CHART

VOLUME MEASUREMENTS (dry)

⅛ teaspoon = 0.5 mL

¼ teaspoon = 1 mL

½ teaspoon = 2 mL

¾ teaspoon = 4 mL

1 teaspoon = 5 mL

1 tablespoon = 15 mL

2 tablespoons = 30 mL

¼ cup = 60 mL

⅓ cup = 75 mL

½ cup = 125 mL

⅔ cup = 150 mL

¼ cup = 175 mL

1 cup = 250 mL

2 cups = 1 pint = 500 mL

3 cups = 750 mL

4 cups = 1 quart = 1 L

VOLUME MEASUREMENTS (fluid)

1 fluid ounce (2 tablespoons) = 30 mL

4 fluid ounces (½ cup) = 125 mL

8 fluid ounces (1 cup) = 250 mL

12 fluid ounces (1½ cups) = 375 mL

16 fluid ounces (2 cups) = 500 mL

WEIGHTS (mass)

½ ounce = 15 g

1 ounce = 30 g

3 ounces = 90 g

4 ounces = 120 g

8 ounces = 225 g

10 ounces = 285 g

12 ounces = 360 g

16 ounces = 1 pound = 450 g

DIMENSIONS

1/16 inch = 2 mm

⅛ inch = 3 mm

¼ inch = 6 mm

½ inch = 1.5 cm

¾ inch = 2 cm

1 inch = 2.5 cm

OVEN TEMPERATURES

250°F = 120°C

275°F = 140°C

300°F = 150°C

325°F = 160°C

350°F = 180°C

375°F = 190°C

400°F = 200°C

425°F = 220°C

450°F = 230°C

BAKING PAN SIZES

Utensil	Size in Inches/ Quarts	Metric Volume	Size in Centimeters
Baking or Cake Pan (square or rectangular)	8×8×2	2 L	20×20×5
	9×9×2	2.5 L	22×22×5
	12×8×2	3 L	30×20×5
	13×9×2	3.5 L	33×23×5
Loaf Pan	8×4×3	1.5 L	20×10×7
	9×5×3	2 L	23×13×7
Round Layer Cake Pan	8×1½	1.2 L	20×4
	9×1½	1.5 L	23×4
Pie Plate	8×1¼	750 mL	20×3
	9×1¼	1 L	23×3
Baking Dish or Casserole	1 quart	1 L	—
	1½ quart	1.5 L	—
	2 quart	2 L	—